Irish Management In

16

Organization Development

Organization Development

A Normative View

W. Warner Burke
*Teachers College, Columbia University
and W. Warner Burke Associates, Inc.*

▲▼ **Addison-Wesley Publishing Company**
*Reading, Massachusetts • Menlo Park, California • Don Mills, Ontario
• Wokingham, England • Amsterdam • Sydney • Singapore • Tokyo
• Madrid • Bogotá • Santiago • San Juan*

This book is in the Addison-Wesley Series on Organization Development.
Editors: Edgar H. Schein, Richard Beckhard

Other titles in the series:

Organizational Transitions:
Managing Complex Change, Second Edition
Richard Beckhard and Reuben Harris

Team Building:
Issues and Alternatives, Second Edition
William G. Dyer

The Technology Connection:
Strategy and Change in the Information Age
Marc S. Gerstein

Stream Analysis:
A Powerful Way to Diagnose and Manage Organizational Change
Jerry I. Porras

Process Consultation Volume II:
Lessons for Managers and Consultants
Edgar H. Schein

Managing Conflict:
Interpersonal Dialogue and Third-Party Roles, Second Edition
Richard E. Walton

Grateful acknowledgment is made to Little, Brown for use of selected material from W. Warner Burke, *Organization Development: Principles and Practices,* pp. 4–12, 20–21, 23–43, 48–51, 153–171, 174–197, 215–217, 334–341, 343–345, 347–350, 352–354, 356–360. Copyright © 1982 by W. Warner Burke. Reprinted by permission of Little, Brown and Company.

Library of Congress Cataloging-in-Publication Data

Burke, W. Warner (Wyatt Warner), 1935–
   Organization development.

   (The Addision-Wesley series on organization development)
   Bibliography: p.
   1. Organizational change.   I. Title.   II. Series.
HD58.8.B878   1987   658.4′06   86–26474
ISBN 0–201–10697–3

ABCDEFGHIJ–BA–8987

To Bobbi

Foreword

The Addison-Wesley Series on Organization Development originated in the late 1960s when a number of us recognized that the rapidly growing field of "OD" was not well understood or well defined. We also recognized that there was no one OD philosophy, and hence one could not at that time write a textbook on the theory and practice of OD, but one could make clear what various practitioners were doing under that label. So the original six books by Beckhard, Bennis, Blake and Mouton, Lawrence and Lorsch, Schein, and Walton launched what has since become a continuing enterprise. The essence of this enterprise was to let different authors speak for themselves instead of trying to summarize under one umbrella what was obviously a rapidly growing and highly diverse field.

By 1981 the series included nineteen titles, having added books by Beckhard and Harris, Cohen and Gadon, Davis, Dyer, Galbraith, Hackman and Oldham, Heenan and Perlmutter, Kotter, Lawler, Nadler, Roeber, Schein, and Steele. This proliferation reflected what had happened to the field of OD. It was growing by leaps and bounds, and it was expanding into all kinds of organizational areas and technologies of intervention. By this time many textbooks existed as well that tried to capture the core concepts of the field, but we felt that diversity and innovation were still the more salient aspects of OD today.

The present series is an attempt both to recapture some basics and to honor the growing diversity. So we have begun a series of revisions of some of the original books and have added a set of new authors or old authors with new content. Our hope is to capture the spirit of inquiry and innovation that has always been the hallmark of organization development and to launch with these books a new wave of insights into the forever tricky problem of how to change and improve organizations.

We are grateful that Addison-Wesley has chosen to continue the series and are also grateful to the many reviewers who have helped us and the authors in the preparation of the current series of books.

Cambridge, Massachusetts   Edgar H. Schein
New York, New York   Richard Beckhard

Preface

My purpose with this book is to provide an overview of the field of organization development (OD). I have written it with at least three audiences in mind: 1) the manager, executive, or administrator—a potential user of organization development; 2) the practitioner in the field of OD—a user who may need some guidelines for practice either as an internal consultant in an organization, or as an external consultant working with a variety of clients; and 3) the student—one who may in the future use the information provided in either role 1 or 2. Some of the nine chapters are more pertinent to the OD practitioner than to the manager. The following synopsis of each chapter will help the reader make choices, should time and interest be limited.

Although I believe that I have been objective in describing OD, the theories underlying the field, and the way OD practitioners typically work, I do represent a bias. I take a position about what I think OD *should* be—thus, the subtitle of the book, "A Normative View." My particular bias is to define OD in part as the change of an organization's culture. Not everyone in the field agrees with me. Moreover, Ed Schein, one of the editors of this Addison-Wesley OD series, has serious doubt that an organization's culture can be changed. Whether you, the reader, believe one way or the other (or whether you even care!) should not prevent a reasonable understanding of how I have described the concepts and practice of organization development.

Chapter 1, "What Is Organization Development?", presents an actual case example of a previous consulting assignment of mine that I believe succinctly illustrates the primary characteristics of OD practice but does not exemplify what OD really is, or should be, taking into consideration my bias.

Chapter 2, "Organization Development Then and Now," provides context for the field by considering OD today, comparing it with the past, and then relating OD to future trends in the organization of tomorrow.

Chapter 3, "Where Did OD Come From?", traces the roots or forerunners of the field and briefly describes ten theories related to organizational behavior that underlie OD practice.

Chapter 4, "Organization Development as a Process of Change," covers the fundamental models of change that guide OD practitioners and, using another actual case for illustration, also covers the phases of consultation that OD practitioners follow in their practice.

Chapter 5, "Understanding Organizations: The Process of Diagnosis," describes some of the most common frameworks or organizational models that OD practitioners use. After conducting interviews, making observations, and perhaps administering some questionnaires and reading some documents, the practitioner attempts to make systematic sense out of what often at first is a mass of confusing data. An organizational model is essential for making sense of the data.

Chapter 6, "Planning and Managing Change," provides an explanation of what OD practitioners do after their diagnostic phase and includes many of the primary steps involved in managing change.

Chapter 7, "Does OD Work?", presents some summary evidence that it does, highlights the issues in evaluating OD efforts, and provides the key reasons for conducting an evaluation.

Chapter 8, "The OD Consultant," covers consultant roles and functions, abilities required and typical needs of an OD practitioner, and how one may become an OD practitioner.

Chapter 9, "Organization Development Now and in the

Future," the final chapter, is both a look to the future and a description of what I consider the essence of OD practice to be by considering the question of "Who is the client?"

Having previously written a textbook on OD (Burke, 1982), I have drawn from it to write this book, especially the parts describing the practice of organization development, including a couple of case examples and explanations of the theories that have contributed to the field.

Richard Beckhard, Frank Friedlander, and Edgar Schein, three of the most experienced and respected persons in OD, were reviewers of the manuscript that eventually became this book. It would be difficult, if not impossible, to have had reviewers who could equal their critique and insight. My sincere appreciation is gratefully offered.

My assistant, Mary Zippo, was invaluable in translating my handwriting to typed page. She has mastered the word processor. I doubt if I ever will, so thank God for Mary!

Pelham, New York   W. Warner Burke

Contents

1

What Is Organization Development?

The term *organization development*, or "OD," the label most commonly used for the field, has been in use since at least 1960. In the 1960s and early 1970s, jokes about what the abbreviation OD meant were common. Today in the world of large organizations, most people would not associate OD with overdose, olive drab, or officer of the day. Organization development as a field may not as yet be sufficiently known to be defined in the dictionary or explained in the *Encyclopaedia Britannica*, but it has survived some turbulent times and, from all appearances, should be around for the foreseeable future. Explaining what OD is and what people do who practice OD continues to be difficult because the field is still being shaped to some degree and because the practice of OD is more of a process than a step-by-step procedure. That is, OD is a consideration in general of how work is done, what the people who carry out the work believe and feel about their efficiency and effectiveness, rather than a specific, concrete, step-by-step linear recipe or algorithm for accomplishing something.

A case example should help to explain. The case represents a fairly strict, purist stance for determining what OD is and what it is not.

A Case Example

The client organization was a division of a large U.S. manufacturing corporation. The division consisted of two plants, both of which manufactured heavy electrical equipment. The division was in trouble at the time. There were quality and control problems and customers were complaining. The complaints concerned not only poor quality but late delivery of these products — inevitably weeks, if not months, later than promised. Several weeks prior to my arrival at the divisional offices, a senior vice-president from the corporation's headquarters had visited with the division's top management team, a group of six men. The corporate vice-president was very much aware of the problems, and he was anything but pleased about the state of affairs. At the end of his visit, he made a pronouncement. In essence, he stated that unless this division was "turned around" within six months, he would make the necessary arrangements to close it down. If he carried through with this threat, it would mean loss of jobs for more than 1000 people, including, of course, the division's top management team. Although the two plants in this division were unionized, the vice-president had the power and the support from his superiors to close the division if he deemed it necessary.

Over a period of several months prior to my arrival as a consultant, the division general manager had taken a variety of steps to try to correct the problems. He had held problem-solving meetings with his top management team; he had fired the head of manufacturing and brought in a more experienced man; he spent time on the shop floor talking with first-line supervisors and workers; he authorized experiments to be conducted by the production engineers to discover better methods; he even conducted a mass rally of all employees at which he exhorted them to do better. After the rally, signs were posted throughout the plants announcing the goal: to become number one among all the corporation's divisions. None of these steps seemed to make any difference.

The general manager also sought help from the corporate staff of employee relations and training specialists. One of these specialists made several visits to the division and eventually decided that an outside consultant with expertise in organization development could probably help. I was contacted by this corporate staff person, and an initial visit was arranged.

My initial visit, only a few weeks after the corporate vice-president had made his visit and his pronouncement, consisted largely of 1) talking at length with the general manager, 2) observing briefly most of the production operations, 3) meeting informally with the top management team so that questions could be raised and issues explored, and finally, 4) discussing the action steps I proposed. I suggested we start at the top. I would interview each member of the top management team at some length and report back to them as a group what I had diagnosed from these interviews; then we would jointly determine the appropriate next steps. They agreed to my proposal.

A couple of weeks later, I began by interviewing the six members of the top management team (see Fig. 1–1) for about an

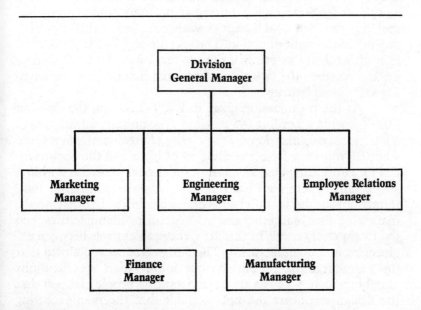

Figure 1–1
Organization Chart: Top Management Team of Manufacturing Division

hour each. They gave many reasons for the division's problems, some of the presumed causes contradicting others. What did emerge was that, although divisional goals were generally understandable, they were not specific enough for clarity about priorities. Moreover, there were interpersonal problems, such as the head of marketing and the head of employee relations not getting along. (The marketing manager believed that the employee relations manager was never forceful enough, and the employee relations manager perceived the marketing manager as a "blowhard.") We decided to have a two-and-a-half-day meeting at a hotel some ninety miles away to work on clarifying priorities and ironing out some of the interpersonal differences.

The meeting was considered successful because much of what we set out to accomplish was achieved — a clearer understanding of the problems and concerns and a priority for action. The key problem needing attention did indeed surface. It was as if a layer or two of an "organizational onion" had been peeled away and we were finally getting at not only some causes but specifics that we could address with confidence that we were moving in the right direction. The specific problem that surfaced from this off-site meeting of the top team was the lack of cooperation between the two major divisional functions — engineering and manufacturing.

As the organization chart in Fig. 1–1 shows, the division was organized according to functions. The primary advantages of a functional organization are the clarity of organizational responsibilities resulting from the division of labor and the opportunities for continuing development of functional expertise within a single unit. There are disadvantages, however, primarily stemming from the distinct divisions of responsibility. In other words, marketing does marketing and manufacturing manufactures, and the twain rarely meet. In this case, the problem was between engineering and manufacturing. The design engineers claimed that the manufacturing people did not follow their specifications closely enough, whereas the manufacturing people claimed that the design engineers did not consider that the manufacturing equipment was old and used. Because of the condition of the machinery, the manufacturing people were not able to follow the design engineers' specifications to the desired tolerance level.

Each group blamed the other for the drop in overall product quality and for the delays in delivery of the product to their customers.

This kind of conflict is common in organizations that are organized functionally. The advantages of such organization are clear, of course, but a premium is placed on the need for cooperation and communication across functional lines. Moreover, when managers are in the midst of such conflict, the pressures of daily production schedules make it difficult for them to pull away and clearly diagnose the situation, especially in terms of what is cause and what is symptom. Managers in high-productivity-oriented organizations thus spend a great deal of time "fighting fires," or treating symptoms. An outside consultant who is not caught up in this day-to-day routine can be more objective in helping to diagnose problem situations. This was my primary role as a consultant to this division.

The next step in my consultative process was to deal with this problem of intergroup conflict. Another off-site meeting was held about a month later with twelve attendees, the top six people from engineering and the equivalent group from manufacturing. These men were predominantly engineers, either design engineers assigned to the engineering function or production engineers working in the manufacturing operation. These two functions had interacted closely, or they were supposed to. The design engineers sent plans (similar to blueprints) to manufacturing to have the specified electrical equipment produced. As noted earlier, the manufacturing people complained that the designers established specifications for tolerances that were significantly more stringent than their machinery could handle. The manufacturing department stated further that the machinery was too old. In order to meet the design specifications, new machinery would have to be purchased, and the cost would be prohibitive. "And besides," they added, "those design guys never set foot on the shop floor anyway, so how would they know?"

These comments and the attitudes they reflect are illustrative and common. Communication is rarely what it should be between groups in such organizations. It is also common, if not natural, for functional groups to maintain a distance from one another and to protect their turfs.

Using a standard intergroup problem-solving format from organization development technology, I worked with the two groups 1) to understand and clarify their differences, 2) to reorganize the two functional groups temporarily into three four-person cross-functional groups to solve problems, and 3) to plan specific action steps they could take to correct their intergroup problems. The purpose of this kind of activity is to provide a procedure for bringing the conflict to the surface so that it can be understood and managed more productively. The procedure begins with an exchange of perceptions between the two functional groups about how each group sees itself and the other group. This initial activity is followed by identifying the problems that exist between the two groups. Finally, mixed groups of members from both functions work together to plan action steps that will alleviate the conflict and solve many of the problems. (See Figure 1–2 for a summary of this process and refer to Burke [1974] for a detailed description of this activity.)

The outcome of this intergroup meeting clearly suggested yet another step. A major problem needing immediate attention was that the manufacturing group was not working well as a team. The design engineers produced evidence that they often got different answers to the same design production problem from different manufacturing people. Thus, the next consulting step was to help conduct a team-building session for the top group of the manufacturing function. Approximately two months after the intergroup session, I met off-site for two days with the production engineers and general foremen of manufacturing. In this session, we set specific manufacturing targets, established production priorities, clarified roles and responsibilities, and even settled a few interpersonal conflicts.

By this time I had been working with the division on and off, from my initial contact, for close to nine months. After my team-building session with the manufacturing group, I was convinced that I had begun to see some of the real causes of the divisional problems; until then I had been dealing primarily with symptoms, not causes. I noticed, for example, that the first-line supervisors had no tangible way of rewarding their hourly workers; they could use verbal strokes — "Nice job, Alice," or "Keep up the good work, Joe" — but that was about it. They could use negative reinforcement, however, if they so chose — for example,

General problem is conflict between:

| Manufacturing department (six people) | Engineering Design department (six people) |

Step 1: Identify Perceptions
Each department of six members working as a group and separately from other departments generates three lists: how we see ourselves, how we see them, and how we think they see us.

Step 2: Exchange of Perceptions
Meeting as total community of twelve yet remaining intact as a department, each group of six presents its lists of perceptions to the other department.

Step 3: Problem Identification
Based on information presented in Step 2, each department of six, again working separately, identifies the primary problems that exist between the two departments.

Step 4: Problem Exchange
Each group presents problem list to the other group.

Step 5: Problem Consolidation
Total group, or representatives from each department, consolidates the two lists into one.

Step 6: Priority Setting
All twelve people rank the problem list from most to least important.

Step 7: Group Problem Solving
Total community is reorganized into three cross-departmental, temporary problem-solving groups. Each of the three groups, consisting of four people, two from manufacturing and two from engineering design, takes one of the top three most important problems and generates solutions.

Step 8: Summary Presentations
Each of the three groups presents its solutions to the other two groups.

Step 9: Follow-Up Planning
Final activity in total community of twelve is to plan implementation steps for problem solutions.

Figure 1–2
Example of Intergroup Problem-Solving Process

threatening a one- or two-week layoff without pay if performance did not meet standards. This type of action was within the bounds of the union contract.

The hourly employees were paid according to what is called a measured day-work system. Their pay was based on what an industrial engineer had specified as an average rate of productivity for a given job during an eight-hour day. Incentive to produce more for extra pay was not part of the system.

I suggested to the division general manager that a change in the reward system might be in order. At that suggestion, the blood seemed to drain from his face. What I then came to understand was that the present president of the corporation was the person who, years before, had invented the measured day-work system. He did not believe in incentive systems. The division general manager made it clear that he was not about to suggest to the corporate president that the measured day-work system should perhaps be scrapped. I discussed this matter with my original corporate contact, the staff specialist. He confirmed the situation and stated that the change in the reward system was not in the offing. I became extremely frustrated at this point. I thought that I had finally hit upon a basic cause of divisional, if not corporate, production problems, but it became apparent that this root of the problem tree was not going to be dug up. My consulting work with the division ended shortly thereafter. What I urged as a next step in the overall problem-solving process — to change some elements of the reward system for hourly employees, if not the entire system — was not a step the division general manager was willing to take. The corporate staff person was also unwilling to push for change in this aspect of the system.

The point of this consultation case is as follows: What I used as a consultant was the standard methodology of organization development, but the project was *not*, in the final analysis, organization development. Having described the case, I will now use it as a vehicle for clarifying what OD is and what it is not.

Definitions

In the consultation, I used OD methodology and approached the situation from an OD perspective. The methodological model for OD is *action research;* data on the nature of certain problems are systematically collected (the research aspect) and then action is taken as a function of what the analyzed data indicate. The specific techniques used within this overall methodological model (few of which are unique to OD) were

1. *Diagnosis.* Interviews with both individuals and groups and observation, followed by analysis and organization of the data collected
2. *Feedback.* Reporting back to those from whom the data were obtained on the collective sense of the organizational problems
3. *Discussion.* Analyzing what the data mean and planning the steps that should be taken as a consequence
4. *Action.* Taking those steps.

In OD language, taking a step is making an *intervention* into the routine way in which the organization operates. In the consultation case there were three primary interventions: team building with the division general manager and the five functional heads who reported directly to him, intergroup conflict resolution between the engineering and manufacturing groups, and team building with the top team of the manufacturing group.

The case does not qualify as an effort in organization development because it meets only two of the three criteria for OD, at least as I have defined them (Burke and Hornstein, 1972). For change in an organization to be OD it must 1) respond to an actual and perceived need for change on the part of the client, 2) involve the client in the planning and implementation of the change, and 3) lead to change in the organization's culture.

As a consultant I was able to meet the first two criteria but not the third. For cultural change to have taken place in this case, the reward system would have to have been modified. In another organization, perhaps, it would not have been the reward system but some other aspect of the culture. Thus, the bias presented in this book is that organization development is a process of fundamental change in an organization's *culture*. By fundamental change, as opposed to fixing a problem or improving a procedure, I mean that some significant aspect of an organization's culture will never be the same. In the case example, it was the reward system. In another case, it might be a change in the organization's management approach or style, requiring new forms of exercising authority, which in turn would lead to different conformity patterns, since new norms would be established, especially in the area of decision making.

Now that we have jumped from a specific case to more general concepts, perhaps we should slow down and define some terms. Any organization, like any society, has its own unique culture. A given culture consists of many elements, but the primary element is the unique pattern of norms, or standards or rules of conduct, to which members conform. Other significant elements of an organization's culture are its authority structure and how power is exercised, values that are unique to the organization, rewards (what they are and how they are dispensed), and communication patterns.

My definition of culture may be somewhat limited, that is, my emphasis, for example, on norms and values. The reasoning behind this way of defining culture is an attempt to understand culture in terms that are operational: conforming patterns of behavior. Norms can be changed. The changed behavior is different conformity. This position, albeit perhaps limited, is nevertheless consistent with Kurt Lewin's thinking concerning change in a social system (Lewin, 1958; see Chapter 3 of this book).

Edgar Schein (1985) defines culture at a "deeper" level:

> *basic assumptions* and *beliefs* that are shared by members of an organization, that operate unconsciously, and that define in a basic "taken-for-granted" fashion an organization's view of itself and its environment. These assumptions and beliefs are *learned* responses to a group's problems of *internal integration*. They come to be taken for granted because they solve those problems repeatedly and reliably. This deeper level of assumptions is to be distinguished from the "artifacts" and "values" that are manifestations or surface levels of the culture but not the essence of the culture. (pp. 6–7)

According to Schein's definition, I am dealing with surface levels. And this is true — almost. The OD practitioner's job is to elicit from the client implicit norms, those conforming patterns that are ubiquitous but are just below the surface, not salient.

These behaviors are *manifestations* of basic assumptions and beliefs as Schein notes, and may not be the essence but constitute more operational means for dealing with organizational change.

For an organization to develop, then, change must occur, but this does not mean that *any* change will do. Using the term *development* to mean change does not, for example, mean growth. Russell Ackoff's distinction is quite useful and relevant to our understanding of what the "D" in OD means:

> Growth can take place with or without development (and vice versa). For example, a cemetery can grow without developing; so can a rubbish heap. A nation, corporation, or an individual can develop without growing. . . . [Development] is an increase in capacity and potential, not an increase in attainment. . . . It has less to do with how much one has than with how much one can do with whatever one has. (Ackoff, 1981, pp. 34, 35)

OD, therefore, is a process of bringing to the surface, that is, to the conscious awareness of the members of an organization, those implicit behavioral patterns that are helping and hindering development. When these patterns of conformity are brought to people's awareness, then they are in a position to reinforce the behaviors that help development and change those that hinder. OD practitioners help clients to help themselves.

More specifically, OD practitioners are concerned with change that will more fully integrate individual needs with organizational goals; change that will lead to greater organizational effectiveness through better utilization of resources, especially human resources; and change that will provide more involvement of organization members in the decisions that directly affect them and their working conditions.

At least by implication and occasionally directly, I shall define OD several times throughout this book. The following definition is somewhat general and perhaps vague, but it provides a starting point: Organization development is a planned process of change in an organization's culture through the utilization of behavioral science technologies, research, and theory.

What if an organization's culture does not need any change? Then OD is neither relevant nor appropriate. Organization development is not all things to all organizations. It is useful only when some fundamental change is needed. Then how does one recognize when fundamental change is needed? Perhaps the clearest sign is when the same kinds of problems keep occurring. No sooner does one problem get solved than another just like it surfaces. Another sign is when a variety of techniques is used to increase productivity, for example, and none seems to work. Yet another is when morale among employees is low and the cause can be attributed to no single factor. There are undoubtedly further questions and more elaboration could be provided, but let us continue.

A Total System Approach

The target for change is the organization — the total system, not necessarily individual members (Burke and Schmidt, 1971). Individual change is typically a consequence of system change. When a norm, a dimension of the organization's culture, is changed, individual behavior is modified by the new conforming pattern. Organization development is a total system approach to change.

Most people who work in OD agree that it is an approach to a total system and that an organization is a sociotechnical system (Trist, 1960). Every organization has a technology, whether it is producing something tangible or rendering a service, and this technology is a subsystem of the total organization and represents an integral part of the culture. Every organization is also composed of people who interact around a task or series of tasks, and this human dimension constitutes the social subsystem. The emphasis of this book is on the social subsystem, but it should be clear that both subsystems and their interaction must be considered in any effort toward organizational change.

The case at the beginning of this chapter illustrates the sociotechnical qualities or dimensions of an organization. The problem between the engineering and manufacturing groups was both a technical one (out-of-date machinery) and a social one (lack of cooperative behavior). The case also illustrates another important point. A cardinal principle or guideline of OD is to begin any consultation with what the client considers to be the problem, with what he or she deems critical, but not necessarily with what the consultant considers important. Later in the consultative effort specific directions for change can be advocated. The consultant begins as facilitator and then gradually moves on to make specific recommendations.

This process of facilitation followed by advocacy is a disputed issue within the field of organization development. Practitioners and academicians in the field of OD are divided according to their views of organization development as a contingent or a normative approach. The contingent camp argues that OD practitioners should facilitate only change, not focus; the client determines the direction of change, and the OD practitioner helps the client get there. The normative camp, significantly smaller, argues that, although the approach to OD should be facilitative at the beginning, before long the practitioner should begin to recommend, if not argue for, specific directions for change. As the reader will no doubt discern from my presentation of the case in this chapter and from the subtitle of this book, I place myself in the normative camp, the minority group. I am taking a position, but I shall make every attempt to be comprehensive and as objective as possible in my coverage of OD.

In the consultative case example, I dealt almost exclusively for more than nine months with what the client considered the central problems and issues. As I became more confident about what I considered to be causal factors rather than symptoms, I began to argue for broader and more directed change. Until then, it was my opinion that we had been putting out fires for the most part, not determining the systematic arsonists. Stated differently, we were fixing problems, not learning how to change, that is, learning a different *way* of solving problems, the essence of OD.

When one takes a position, regardless of how authoritative, the risk is one of encountering resistance. As is obvious from my description of the case, I didn't consult much longer than the first nine months. The total time was about a year. As it turned out, I did help; the division did turn around in time to keep the corporate vice-president from acting on his threat. As a consultant, I take satisfaction in this outcome. From an OD perspective, however, I consider that my work was a failure. That assessment stems from two perspectives, one concerning research and the other concerning values.

Research evidence regarding organizational change is now very clear. Change rarely if ever can be effected by treating symptoms, and organizational change will not occur if effort is directed at trying to change individual members. The direction of change should be toward the personality of the organization, not the personality of the individual. My knowledge of the research evidence, my realization in the consultation case that a modification in the organization's reward system was not likely, and my acceptance that OD, by definition, means change led me to conclude that, in the final analysis, I had not conducted an organization development effort.

The values that underlie organization development include humanistic and collaborative approaches to changing organizational life. Although all OD practitioners do not agree, an effort at decentralizing power is also included in OD for most organizations. In the consultation case, it seemed that providing first-line supervisors with more alternatives for rewarding their workers positively not only was more humanistic but would allow them more discretionary and appropriate power and authority for accomplishing their supervisory responsibilities. Changing the reward system was the appropriate avenue as far as I was concerned, but this change was not to be and, for my part, neither was OD.

What I have just stated is likely to raise many more questions than answers. Let us move on now to more clarity and, I hope, answers. In the next chapter, we shall explore a broader context for OD as a way of clarifying further the work of OD practitioners and the domain of their work for the future.

2

Organization Development
Then and Now

The original Addison-Wesley OD series, published in 1969, consisted of six volumes. These books represented one of the first attempts to define the field of organization development, the field at the time being at most a decade old. It is now almost two decades later. Let us consider what has happened since 1969 that has had particular relevance for and impact on the field of OD and what the future trends in organizations might be.

Some Significant Changes Since 1969

Perhaps the most significant event that has affected the field of OD since 1969, at least from the perspective of economics if not competence, was the oil embargo and recession of 1972–73. Organizations cut back, especially in the so-called soft areas of training and human resource development. Many who at the time labeled themselves as OD consultants had to change labels. The less experienced and less competent practitioners in the field were "weeded out." Today people in OD, especially those who were involved in the late 1960s and early 1970s and survived the economically tough times of 1973 and after and remain in OD today, are more competent. More people today who call them-selves OD practitioners have either come through tougher times and survived or have taken advantage of the greater accumulated knowledge and learned more quickly the concepts and skills required to practice OD effectively. In either case we seem to have a more competent and definitely a larger group of practitioners today than was true fifteen to twenty years ago.

With respect to organizational dynamics and approaches to management in general, there have been at least six significant shifts since 1969.

First, emphasis shifted from strategic planning to strategic implementation. In 1969 and even more after 1973 strategic planning was emphasized. What was gradually learned was that the planning is only 10% of the job; the other 90% is implementing the plan, the tougher part of the job by far. Thus, managing change is more of the emphasis today.

Second, the terms *organizational culture* and *values* were barely mentioned in 1969. Today these terms are used as often by the client as by the OD consultant. I can remember using the term *culture* in the early 1970s. It didn't exactly "communicate," much less "catch on." Today there is greater clarity and accept-ance of these concepts as critically important to understand in trying to manage, lead, and especially to change an organization. It seems clear today that unless culture change is paired with a significant change in the organization's strategy, ultimately the new strategy will fail. The books by Deal and Kennedy (1982) and Peters and Waterman (1982) paved the way for these shifts in con-ceptual ways of considering an organization.

Third, participation in management, employee involve-ment, and related activities were not endorsed much less em-phasized in 1969. Today, the opposite is true. Many causal factors for this shift could be listed, no doubt. Two stand out: the influ-ence of Japanese management, with its more participative ap-proach, and the changing nature of the U.S. workforce, which is now more educated than formerly, more demanding, less tolerant of any perceived arbitrary use of authority, and more oriented toward professionalism in work (see, for example, Raelin, 1987).

Fourth, while conflict resolution and effectiveness in lateral relations were acknowledged as important in 1969, they are viewed by most executives as critical for effective organizational functioning today. This shift is due in part to 1) more decentralized authority and flatter hierarchies, where getting work done depends more on influence skills than on the exercise of power as a function of position or status, 2) the emphasis being given to collaborative, joint approaches to labor–management relations as opposed to adversarial ones, and 3) the occurrence of mergers and acquisitions, where achieving integration or at least some degree of smooth working relationships is important.

Fifth, in 1969 leadership was not mentioned very often. It was not considered unimportant, but the term simply was seldom used. Today, leadership and its distinctions from management are discussed and debated frequently. The leadership function is not only highlighted more today, it is especially emphasized in the context of bringing about organizational change (see, for example, Tichy and Devanna, 1986).

The sixth shift is more specific to the practice of OD than to management or organizational dynamics in general. OD practitioners have shifted their perspective from a micro to a macro view. In the 1960s organizational issues were viewed mostly in terms of individuals and small groups (sensitivity training, T-groups, management development), whereas today OD practitioners take a larger, more systemic perspective (reward systems, strategic planning, structure, management information systems). This shift is far more realistic for purposes of organizational change.

These six shifts are not the only ones since 1969, but they represent the most significant ones for organization development. OD practitioners are in the business of change and the involvement of people in decisions and activities that directly affect them. These six shifts concern in one way or the other organization change and differences in the ways people are managed.

One other point about change since 1969 should be made. OD practitioners have been fairly naive about and reluctant to deal with power and politics in organizations. Even though OD practitioners today may not be the most skillful people in the world when it comes to dealing with power and politics, they are more willing to accept these organizational dynamics as realities, and more willing to attempt to take them into account when facilitating the management of change.

The New Corporation

To broaden the context regarding changes since 1969 let us consider the work of three current and highly popular writers on the organizational scene, John Naisbett, Tom Peters, and Rosabeth Moss Kanter. Naisbett's *Megatrends (1982)* was indeed a bestseller and caused readers to think about the changing nature of organizations. His later book, co-authored with Patricia Aburdene (Naisbett and Aburdene, 1985), was more to the point of organizational shifts, however. The following is a list of their observations of how today's corporation is being "re-invented":

1. The best and brightest people gravitate toward those corporations that foster personal growth.
2. The manager's role is that of coach, teacher, and mentor.
3. The best people want ownership, both psychic and literal, in a company; the best companies are providing it.
4. Companies are increasingly turning to third-party contractors, shifting from hired labor to contract labor.
5. Authoritarian management is yielding to networking, democratic management.
6. Entrepreneurship within the corporations, sometimes called "intrapreneurship," is creating new products and services that revitalize companies inside out.
7. Quality will be paramount.
8. Intuition and creativity are challenging the "It's all in the numbers" business school philosophy.
9. Large corporations are emulating the positive and productive qualities of small business.
10. The dawn of the information economy has fostered a massive shift from infrastructure to quality of life.

Tom Peters, another astute observer of the organizational scene, has covered the significant shifts he sees in the ways corporations do their business today. He has discussed these shifts in terms of "old to new" across the primary organizational functions. Table 2–1 is a summary of his observations (Peters, 1987).

The third observer and researcher of organizations, Rosabeth Moss Kanter, has been especially interested in managing innovation. In *The Change Masters* (1984), she writes about her findings of innovative practices and patterns across a number of organizations. Pertinent to our consideration here, she lists eight characteristics of innovative organizations:

1. Work responsibilities described in terms of results, with flexibility in the way they are achieved
2. Unallocated resources, such as time or money, available for projects beyond formal job descriptions and business plans
3. Abundant and visible recognition are given for a variety of achievements, not just a few occasional awards for superstars
4. Ongoing budgets for frequent and continuing education and training, plus special assignments that challenge and stretch people
5. An emphasis on communicating business plans, market conditions, and other information through all levels, with advance warning of possible policy shifts
6. Lots of cross-fertilization, with opportunities to transfer into a variety of departments or business units
7. A networking structure, through special project teams, to bring together people at various levels in different departments or business units
8. Frequent trials of new concepts and new ideas, with most people involved in and committed to at least one new initiative a year

Summary

All of these observers and researchers of organizations, Naisbett and Aburdene, Peters, and Kanter, believe that effective organizations have the following characteristics:

Table 2–1
Shifts of Organizational Culture over Time

Old	New

Manufacturing

Old	New
Emphasis on volume, low cost, and efficiency more important than quality and responsiveness; capital and automation more important than people	Emphasis on short production runs; people as important or more so than capital and automation; quality and responsiveness critical; manufacturers as business team members, not just functional specialists; joint problem solving with suppliers

Marketing

Old	New
Mass marketing, advertising, and data analysis; lengthy market tests, highly competitive to achieve market share, analysis over intuition, consideration of large projects only	Fragmented markets, new uses; market creation rather than market sharing; rapid data collection; marketers in the field; innovations via listening to customers; heightened awareness of *service*

Sales and Service

Old	New
Move the product; volume is king; product ideas from marketing and engineering, not sales; service as mechanics, not primary source of customer listening	Sales as relationship management higher priority than volume; sales and service prime input to new product and new service development

International

Old	New
Adjunct activity; way to move post-peak U.S. designated and manufactured products; "global brands" managed by U.S. headquarters marketers	Primary activity; focus on new market creation not just lagging follow-up use of U.S. product; extensive off-shore product development; more mandatory overseas assignments

Table 2–1 (*cont.*)

Old	New

Innovation

Central R&D as driver; big products the norm; technology science driven, not market/customer driven. Cleverness of design more important than reliability, maintainability, and serviceability

All activities represent potential for innovation—manufacturing, management information systems (MIS), personnel, accounting—big ends from small beginnings; flatter, more responsive organizations, all functions to the field, with customers, multifunction teams as opportunity creators

People

Capital more important than people; scale economies the priority; no way to beat turnover problem, therefore training is a waste; unions a dragging force; money is only motivator; employee share ownership only works when stock price is rising

Quality service and responsiveness through people more than through capital; participation programs; gain-sharing programs; extensive training

Organization

Hierarchical, staff centered; officially matrixed to solve coordination needs; span of control 1:10 at the lowest levels

Flat, large span; 1:100; line dominated; business team, group focused smaller facility sizes (250 instead of 1000 people); strategy making bottom-up, decentralized; no group executives

MIS

Centralized information control; central MIS fiefdom as information hoarders for the sake of "consistency"

Decentralized data processing connected by local area networks with access to all other data banks; central MIS as staff advisers for the strategic use of information, for example direct customer-supplier-company linkage

(*continued*)

Table 2–1 *(cont.)*

Old	New
Financial Management and Control	
Centralized; staff as reviewer of all proposals; formulator of extensive guidance—staff as the police	Decentralized; almost all financial people in the field; finance members of business team and entrepreneurial "skunk works"; high-spending authority at facility/business unit level
Leadership	
Detached, analytic; centralized strategy planning dominated by central corporate and group executive staffs	Values set from top, strategic development from below; all staff functions decentralized; value driven; leader as dramatist/tone setter/visionary

- They are less hierarchical in structural terms and "network" more to get work done and to communicate.
- They involve organizational members in decisions they are expected to implement.
- They are, in general, more people oriented.

Both Peters and Kanter stress the importance of three qualities: 1) flexibility in how work is done, that is, allowing as much autonomy as possible, 2) everyone being an innovator, and 3) greater information flow. Naisbett and Aburdene also overlap with Kanter in highlighting the increased emphasis on providing development opportunities and activities for organizational members.

If we consider the points of overlap and agreement among these organizational observers and researchers as strong indicators of organizational effectiveness today and in the near future, and if I am reasonably accurate about the six shifts that have occurred over the last couple of decades, then OD practitioners have a bright and exciting future.

People identified with the field of organization development have consistently been advocates of involving people in decisions that directly affect them. Trends are now more supportive of this position. From a philosophical and value standpoint, OD practitioners have been identified with humanistic means of dealing with members of organizations. Trends are now more supportive of these approaches and values. OD practitioners, being process oriented, have been identified with more flexible ways of communicating and conducting work, have facilitated networking activities, and have been advocates of personal development and growth for organizational members.

It should be clear, after reading the next chapter, that OD's history and theoretical roots are closely linked to much of what is being advocated by observers and researchers of organizational effectiveness today.

3

Where Did OD Come From?

Determining the moment of birth of organization development is not a simple, clear-cut matter. *Evolution* would be a better term than *birth* to characterize the beginnings of OD. The purpose of this chapter, therefore, is to trace briefly the evolution of OD both in terms of certain forerunners, such as sensitivity training, and in terms of selected theoretical roots.

Before OD

Even though OD may be characterized as evolutionary with respect to the field's beginnings, we must start somewhere. There was not a "big bang" or "blessed event." Thus, considering three forerunners or precursors will help us to understand the beginnings, that is, where OD came from. These three precursors are sensitivity training, sociotechnical systems, and survey feedback.

Sensitivity Training

From an historical perspective, it would be interesting to know how many events, inventions, and innovations that occurred around 1946 had lasting impact through the subsequent decades. Apparently once World War II was over, people were somehow freer to pursue a variety of creative endeavors. Both sensitivity training, later "housed" at the National Training Laboratories (NTL), and a similar yet different version of human relations training, independently founded at the Tavistock Institute in London, began about that time.

On the U.S. side, sensitivity training, or the T-group, as it was to be labeled later (T meaning training), derived from events that took place in the summer of 1946 in New Britain, Connecticut. Kurt Lewin, at the time on the faculty of Massachusetts Institute of Technology (MIT) and director of the Research Center for Group Dynamics, was asked by the director of the Connecticut State Inter-Racial Commission to conduct a training workshop that would help to improve community leadership in general and interracial relationships in particular. Lewin brought together a group of colleagues and students to serve as trainers (Leland Bradford, Ronald Lippitt, and Kenneth Benne) and researchers (Morton Deutsch, Murray Horwitz, Arnold Meier, and Melvin Seeman) for the workshop. The training consisted of lectures, role playing, and general group discussion. In the evenings, most researchers and trainers met to evaluate the training to that point by discussing participant behavior as they had observed it during the day. A few of the participants who were far enough from their homes to stay in the dormitory rooms at the college in New Britain asked if they could observe the evening staff discussions. The trainers and researchers were reluctant, but Lewin saw no reason to keep them away and thought that, as participants, they might learn even more.

The results were influential and far-reaching, to say the least. In the course of the staff's discussion of the behavior of one participant, who happened to be present and observing, the participant intervened and said that she disagreed with their interpretations of her behavior. She then described the event from her point of view. Lewin immediately recognized that this intrusion provided a richness to the data collection and analysis that was otherwise unavailable. The next evening many more participants stayed to observe the staff discussions. Observations alone didn't last, of course, and three-way discussions occurred among the researchers, trainers, and participants. Gradually, the staff and participants discovered that the feedback the participants were receiving about their daytime behavior was teaching them as much or more than the daytime activities. The participants were becoming more sensitive to their own behavior in terms of how they were being perceived by others and the impact their behavior was having on others. This serendipitous and innovative mode of learning, which had its beginning that summer in Connecticut, has become what Carl Rogers labeled "perhaps the most significant social invention of the century" (1968: p. 265).

Sensitivity training, T-groups, and laboratory training are all labels for the same process, consisting of small group discussions in which the primary, almost exclusive, source of information for learning is the behavior of the group members themselves. Participants receive feedback from one another regarding their behavior in the group, and this feedback becomes the learning source for personal insight and development. Participants also have an opportunity to learn more about group behavior and intergroup relationships.

T-groups are educational vehicles for change, in this case individual change. During the late 1950s, when this form of education began to be applied in industrial settings for organizational change, the T-group became one of the earliest so-called interventions of organization development.

As the T-group method of learning and change began to proliferate in the 1950s, it naturally gravitated to organizational life. Sensitivity training began to be used as an intervention for organizational change; in this application the training was conducted inside a single organization, and members of the small T-groups were either organizational "cousins" — from the same overall organization but not within the same vertical chain of the organization's hierarchy — or members of the same organizational team, so-called family groups. As French and Bell (1978) reported, one of the first events to improve organizational effectiveness by sensitivity training took place with managers at some of the major refineries of Exxon (then known as Esso) in Louisiana and southeast Texas. Herbert Shepard of the corporate employee relations department and Harry Kolb of the refineries division used interviews followed by three-day training laboratories for all managers in an attempt to move management in a more participative direction. Outside trainers were used, many of them the major names of the National Training Laboratories at the time, such as Lee Bradford and Robert R. Blake. Paul Buchanan conducted similar activities when he was with the Naval Ordnance Test Station at China Lake, California. He later joined Shepard at Esso.

At about that time, Douglas McGregor of the Sloan School of Management at MIT was conducting similar training sessions at Union Carbide. These events at Esso and Union Carbide represented the early forms of organization development, which usually took the form of what we now call team building (Burck, 1965; McGregor, 1967).

Also during that period, the late 1950s, McGregor and Richard Beckhard were consulting with General Mills. They were fostering what now would be called a sociotechnical systems change. They helped to change some of the work structures at the various plants so that more teamwork and increased decision making took place on the shop floor; more bottom-up management began to occur. They didn't want to call what they were doing "bottom-up," nor were they satisfied with "organization development." This label also became, apparently independently, the name for the work Shepard, Kolb, Blake, and others were doing at the Humble Refineries of Esso.

Even though McGregor and Beckhard were initiating organizational change that involved a sociotechnical perspective, they called what they were doing organization development rather than sociotechnical systems. Across the Atlantic at the Tavistock Institute, the sociotechnical label stuck.

Sociotechnical Systems

In the United Kingdom at about the same time that sensitivity began in the United States, Eric Trist and Ken Bamforth of the Tavistock Institute were consulting with a coal mining company. Prior to their consultative intervention, coal was mined by teams of six workers. Each team selected its own members and performed all of the work necessary, from extraction of the coal to loading to getting it above ground. Teams were paid on the basis of group effort and unit productivity, not individual effort. Teams tended to be quite cohesive.

Problems arose when new equipment and a change in technology were introduced. With this introduction a consequent change in the way work was conducted occurred. Rather than group work, individualized labor became the norm. Work therefore became both more individualized and specialized; that is, jobs were more fractionated. Gradually, productivity decreased and absenteeism increased.

Trist and Bamforth suggested a new approach that combined the essential social elements of the previous mode of work — team as opposed to individualized effort — yet retained the new technology. As a consequence of the company's management implementing what Trist and Bamforth suggested, productivity rose to previous levels, if not higher, and absenteeism significantly decreased. The specifics of this early work, including the documented measurements and outcomes are reported in Trist (1960) and Trist and Bramforth (1951).

Shortly thereafter, A. K. Rice, another Tavistock consultant and researcher, conducted similar experiments and changes in two textile mills in Ahmedabad, India. The results of his interventions, which involved combining important social factors while, again, maintaining a group effort with the technological changes, were much the same: increased productivity and reduced damage and costs (Rice, 1958).

The approach pioneered by Trist, Bamforth, Rice, and their colleagues at Tavistock is based on the premise that an organization is simultaneously a social and a technical system. All organizations have a technology, whether it is producing something tangible or rendering a service, and this technology is a subsystem of the total organization. All organizations also are composed of people who interact to perform a task or series of tasks, and this human dimension constitutes the social subsystem. The emphasis of OD is typically on the social subsystem, but both subsystems and their interaction must be considered in any effort toward organizational change.

Survey Feedback

Organization development has been influenced by industrial or organizational psychology. This influence is perhaps manifested most in the third precursor to OD, survey feedback. Industrial or organizational psychologists rely rather extensively on questionnaires for data collection and for diagnosis and assessment. Leadership questionnaires, for example, typically have been associated with the group of psychologists at Ohio State University in the 1950s. Questionnaires for organizational diagnosis, however, are more likely to be associated with the psychologists of the 1950s and 1960s at the Institute for Social Research at the University of Michigan. Rensis Likert, the first director of the institute, started by founding the Survey Research Center in 1946. Kurt Lewin had founded the Research Center for Group Dynamics at MIT. With his untimely death in 1947, the Center was moved to the University of Michigan later that year. These two centers initially constituted Likert's institute. The two primary thrusts of these centers, questionnaire surveys for organizational diagnosis and group dynamics, combined to give birth to the survey feedback method. As early as 1947 questionnaires were being used systematically to assess employee morale and attitudes in organizations.

One of the first of these studies, initiated and guided by Likert and conducted by Floyd Mann, was done with the Detroit Edison Company. From working on the problem of how best to use the survey data for organization improvement, the method now known as survey feedback evolved. Mann was key to the development of this method. He noted that, when a manager was given the survey results, any resulting improvement depended on what the manager did with the information. If the manager discussed the survey results with his or her subordinates, however, and failed to plan certain changes for improvement jointly with them, nothing happened — except, perhaps, an increase in employee frustration with the ambiguity of having answered a questionnaire and never hearing anything further.

Briefly, the survey feedback method involves two steps. The first is the survey, collecting data by questionnaire to determine employees' perceptions of a variety of factors, most focusing on the management of the organization. The second step is the feedback, reporting the results of the survey systematically in summary form to all people who answered the questionnaire. Systematically, in this case, means that feedback occurs in phases, starting with the top team of the organization and flowing downward according to the formal hierarchy and within functional units or teams. Mann (1957) referred to this flow as the "interlocking chain of conferences." The chief executive officer, the division general manager, or the bureau chief, depending on the organization or subunit surveyed, and his or her immediate group of subordinates receive and discuss feedback from the survey first. Next, the subordinates and their respective groups of immediate subordinates do the same, and so forth downward until all members of the organization who had been surveyed hear a summary of the survey and then participate in a discussion of the meaning of the data and the implications. Each functional unit of the organization receives general feedback concerning the overall organization and specific feedback regarding its particular group. Following a discussion of the meaning of the survey results for their particular groups, boss and subordinates then jointly plan action steps for improvement. Usually, a consultant meets with each of the groups to help with data analysis, group discussion, and plans for improvement.

This is a rather orderly and systematic way of understanding an organization from the standpoint of employee perceptions and processing this understanding back into the organization so that change can occur, with the help of an outside resource person. Not only was it a direct precursor to and root of organization development, but it is an integral part of many current OD efforts.

Current OD efforts using survey feedback methodology do not, however, always follow a top-down, cascading process. The survey may begin in the middle of the managerial hierarchy and flow in either or both directions, or may begin at the bottom and work upward, as Edgar Schein (1969) has suggested. For more information about and guidelines for conducting survey feedback activities, see David Nadler's book in the Addison-Wesley OD series (Nadler, 1977).

Finally, it should be noted that there are other forerunners or precursors to OD. A case in point is the activity prior to World War II at the Hawthorne Works of Western Electric. There the work of Mayo (1933), Roethlisberger and Dickson (1939), and Homans (1950) established that psychological and sociological factors make significant differences in worker performance.

The work at Hawthorne and its consequent popularity and impact occurred some two decades prior to the three precursors I chose to discuss in some depth. Thus, sensitivity training, sociotechnical systems, and survey feedback had a much greater and more direct influence on the beginnings of OD.

Theoretical Roots

Organization development has other roots in the area of concepts, models, and theories. Some people in or related to the burgeoning field of OD in the 1960s not only were doing but were thinking and writing as well. Some took an individual viewpoint, others a group perspective, and still others more of a macro view with the total organization as the frame of reference.

What follows is a synopsis of some of the thinking of a fairly select group of people who have helped to provide most of the theoretical and conceptual underpinnings of organization development. Ten theorists or conceptualizers were selected to represent the theory that is associated with organization development, because no single theory or conceptual model is representative or by itself encompasses the conceptual field or the practice of OD. What we have now is a group of minitheories that have influenced the thinking and consultative practice of OD practitioners. I refer to them as minitheories because each helps to explain only a portion of organizational behavior and effectiveness.

The ten theories or theory categories were selected because they best represent the theory we do have within the field of OD. Some prominent names in the field of OD were not included because their contributions have been more descriptive than theoretical, such as Blake and Mouton's (1978) Managerial Grid, a model of managerial styles; more practice-oriented, such as Beckhard (1969); Schein (1969); and Walton (1969); or more broadly explanatory and provocative, such as Bennis (1966, 1967, 1969, 1970). The selection is a matter of judgment and certainly could be debated. Moreover, some of these theorists would not consider themselves to be OD practitioners. In fact, I have heard Frederick Herzberg state that he did not associate himself with the field.

B. F. Skinner may never have heard of organization development. In other words, these theorists did not elect themselves into OD. I have chosen them because I believe that their thinking has had a large impact on the practices of OD.

The ten theories are presented in three major categories:

- The individual approach to change (Maslow and Herzberg, expectancy theorists Vroom and Lawler, job satisfaction theorists Hackman and Oldham, and Skinner)
- T-group approach to change (Lewin, Argyris, and Bion)
- The total system approach to change (Likert, Lawrence and Lorsch, and Levinson)

Individual Perspective

Psychologists have taken two major approaches to the understanding of human motivation: need theory and expectancy theory. One of the early proponents of need theory was Murray; later representatives were Maslow and Herzberg. Expectancy theory, a more recent approach to understanding human motivation, is usually associated with Lawler and Vroom. Applications of need theory in organizations have centered around job design, career development, and certain aspects of human relations training, whereas expectancy theory has been applied with respect to both needs and rewards systems.

Need Theory — Maslow and Herzberg

According to Maslow (1954), human motivation can be explained in terms of needs that people experience in varying degrees all the time. An unsatisfied need creates a state of tension, which releases energy in the human system and, at the same time, provides direction. This purposeful energy guides the individual toward some goal that will respond to the unsatisfied need. The process whereby an unsatisfied need provides energy and direction toward some goal is Maslow's definition of motivation. Thus, only unsatisfied needs provide the sources of motivation; a satisfied need creates no tension and therefore no motivation.

Maslow contended that we progress through this five-level

need system in a hierarchical fashion and that we do so one level at a time. The hierarchy represents a continuum from basic or psychological needs to safety and security needs to belongingness needs to ego-status needs to a need for self-actualization.

It is on this last point, a single continuum, that Herzberg parts company with Maslow. Herzberg (1966; Herzberg, Mausner, and Snyderman, 1959) maintains that there are two continua, one concerning dissatisfaction and the other concerning satisfaction. It may be that the two theorists are even more fundamentally different in that Herzberg's approach has more to do with job satisfaction than with human motivation. The implications and applications of the two are much more similar than they are divergent, however.

Specifically, Herzberg argues that only the goal objects associated with Maslow's ego-status and self-actualization needs provide motivation or satisfaction on the job. Meeting the lower-order needs simply reduces dissatisfaction; it does not provide satisfaction. Herzberg calls the goal objects associated with these lower-level needs (belonging, safety, and basic) hygiene or maintenance factors. Providing fringe benefits, for example, prevents dissatisfaction and thus is hygienic, but this provision does not ensure job satisfaction. Only motivator factors, such as recognition, opportunity for achievement, and autonomy on the job ensure satisfaction.

Herzberg's two categories, motivator factors and maintenance or hygiene factors, do not overlap. They represent qualitatively different aspects of human motivation.

It is important to note one other point of Herzberg's. He states that not only does the dimension of job dissatisfaction differ psychologically from job satisfaction, but it is also associated with an escalation phenomenon, or what some have called the principle of rising expectations: the more people receive, the more they want. This principle applies only to job dissatisfaction. Herzberg uses the example of a person who receives a salary increase of $1000 one year and then receives only a $500 increase the following year. Psychologically, the second increase is a cut in pay. Herzberg maintains that this escalation principle is a fact of life, and that we must live with it. Management must continue to provide, upgrade, and increase maintenance factors — good working conditions, adequate salaries, and competitive fringe benefits — but should not operate under the false assumption that these factors will lead to greater job satisfaction.

Job enrichment, a significant intervention within OD and a critical element of quality-of-work-life projects, is a direct application of Herzberg's theory and at least an indirect one of Maslow's.

Expectancy Theory — Lawler and Vroom

Expectancy theory (Lawler, 1973; Vroom, 1964) has yet to have the impact on organization development that need theory has had, but it is gaining in acceptance and popularity. This approach to understanding human motivation focuses more on outward behavior than on internal needs. The theory is based on three assumptions:

1. People believe that their behavior is associated with certain outcomes. Theorists call this belief the *performance-outcome expectancy*. People may expect that if they accomplish certain tasks, they will receive certain rewards.
2. Outcomes or rewards have different values (*valence*) for different people. Some people, for example, are more attracted to money as a reward than others are.
3. People associate their behavior with certain probabilities of success, called the *effort-performance expectancy*. People on an assembly line, for example, may have high expectancies that, if they try, they can produce 100 units per hour, but their expectancies may be very low that they can produce 150 units, regardless of how hard they may try.

Thus, people will be highly motivated when they believe 1) that their behavior will lead to certain rewards, 2) that these rewards are worthwhile and valuable, and 3) that they are able to perform at a level that will result in the attainment of the rewards.

Research has shown that high-performing employees believe that their behavior, or performance, leads to rewards that they desire. Thus, there is evidence for the validity of the theory.

Moreover, the theory and the research outcomes associated with it have implications for how reward systems and work might be designed and structured.

Job Satisfaction — Hackman and Oldham

Hackman and Oldham's (1980) *work design model* is grounded in both need theory and expectancy theory. Their model is more restrictive in that it focuses on the relationship between job or work design and worker satisfaction. Although their model frequently leads to what is called job enrichment, as does the application of Herzberg's motivator-hygiene theory, the Hackman and Oldham model has broader implications. Briefly, Hackman and Oldham (1975) contend that there are three primary psychological states that significantly affect worker satisfaction:

1. Experienced meaningfulness of the work itself
2. Experienced responsibility for the work and its outcomes
3. Knowledge of results, or performance feedback

The more that work is designed to enhance these states, the more satisfying the work will be.

Positive Reinforcement — Skinner

The best way to understand the full importance of the applications of B. F. Skinner's (1953, 1971) thinking and his research results is to read his novel, *Walden Two* (1948). The book is about a utopian community designed and maintained according to Skinnerian principles of operant behavior and schedules of reinforcement. A similar application was made in an industrial situation in the Emery Air Freight case ("At Emery," 1973). By applying Skinnerian principles, which are based on numerous research findings, Emery quickly realized an annual savings of $650,000. (The Emery case is discussed more fully later in this section.)

Skinner is neither an OD practitioner nor a management consultant, but his theory and research are indeed applicable to management practices and to organizational change. For Skinner, control is key. If one can control the environment, one can then control behavior. In Skinner's approach, the more the environment is controlled the better, but the necessary element of control is the reward, both positive and negative. This necessity is based on a fundamental of behavior that Skinner derived from his many years of research, a concept so basic that it may be a law of behavior, that people (and animals) do what they are rewarded for doing. Let us consider the principles that underlie this fundamental of behavior.

The first phase of learned behavior is called *shaping*, the process of successive approximations to reinforcement. When children are learning to walk, they are reinforced by their parents' encouraging comments or physical stroking, but this reinforcement typically follows only the behaviors that lead to effective walking. *Programmed learning*, invented by Skinner, is based on this principle. To maintain the behavior, a schedule of reinforcement is applied and, generally, the more variable the schedule is, the longer the behavior will last.

Skinner therefore advocates positive reinforcement for shaping and controlling behavior. Often, however, when we consider controlling behavior, we think of punishment ("If you don't do this, you're gonna get it!"). According to Skinner, punishment is no good. His stance is not based entirely on his values or whims, however. Research clearly shows that, although punishment may temporarily stop a certain behavior, negative reinforcement must be administered continuously for this certain process to be maintained. The principle is the opposite of that for positively reinforced behavior. There are two very practical concerns here. First, having to reinforce a certain behavior continuously is not very efficient. Second, although the punished behavior may be curtailed, it is unlikely that the subject will learn what to do; all that is learned is what *not* to do.

Thus, the way to control behavior according to Skinnerian theory and research is to reinforce the desirable behavior positively and, after the shaping process, to reinforce the behavior only occasionally. An attempt should be made to ignore undesirable behavior and not to punish (unless, perhaps, society must be protected) but, rather, to spend time positively shaping the desired behavior. The implications of Skinner's work for organizations is that a premium is placed on such activities as establishing incentive systems, reducing or eliminating many of the control systems that contain inherent threats and punishments, providing feedback to all levels of employees regarding their performance, and developing programmed-learning techniques for training employees.

The application of Skinner's work to OD did not occur systematically until the 1970s. Thus, his influence is not as pervasive as is Maslow's, for example. Skinner's behavior-motivation techniques as applied to people also raise significant questions regarding ethics and values: Who exercises the control, and is the recipient aware? Thus, it is not a question of whether Skinner's methodology works, but rather how and under what circumstances it is used.

Group Perspective

The Group as the Focus of Change — Lewin

The theorist among theorists, at least within the scope of the behavioral sciences, is Kurt Lewin. His thinking has had a more pervasive impact on organization development, both directly and indirectly, than any other person's. It was Lewin who laid the groundwork for much of what we know about social change, particularly in a group and by some extrapolation in an organization. Lewin's interest and, easily determined by implication, his values have also influenced OD. As a Jew who escaped Hitler's Germany in the 1930s, it was not coincidental that Lewin was intensely interested in the study of autocratic versus democratic behavior and matters of influence and change (Marrow, 1969). Thus, his own and his students' research findings regarding the consequences of such variables as participative leadership and decision making have had considerable impact on the typical objectives of most if not all OD efforts.

According to Lewin (1948, 1951), behavior is a function of a person's personality, discussed primarily in terms of motivation or needs, and the situation or environment in which the person is acting. The environment is represented as a field of forces that affect the person. Thus, a person's behavior at any given moment can be predicted if we know that person's needs and if we can determine the *intensity* and *valence* (whether the force is positive or negative for the person) of the forces impinging on the person from the environment. Although Lewin borrowed the term *force* from physics, he defined the construct psychologically. Thus, one's perception of the environment is key, not necessarily reality. An example of a force, therefore, could be the perceived power of another person. Whether or not I will accomplish a task you want me to do is a function of the degree to which such accomplishment will respond to a need I have and how I perceive your capacity to influence me — whether you are a force in my environment (field).

Lewin made a distinction between *imposed* or induced forces, those acting on a person from the outside, and *own* forces, those directly reflecting the person's needs. The implications of this distinction are clear. Participation in determining a goal is more likely to create its own forces toward accomplishing it than is a situation in which goal determination is imposed by others. When a goal is imposed on a person, his or her motives may match accomplishment of the goal, but the chances are considerably more variable or random than if the goal is determined by the person in the first place. Typically, then, for imposed or induced goals to be accomplished by a person, the one who induced them must exert continuous influence or else the person's other motives, not associated with goal accomplishment, will likely determine his or her behavior. This aspect of Lewin's theory helps to explain the generally positive consequences of participative management and consensual decision making.

Another distinction Lewin made regarding various forces in a person's environment is the one between *driving* and *restraining* forces. Borrowing yet another concept from physics, quasi-stationary equilibria, he noted that the perceived status quo in life is just that — a *perception*. In reality, albeit psychological reality, a given situation is a result of a dynamic process and is not static. The process flows from one moment to the next, with ups and downs, and over time gives the impression of a static situation, but there actually are some forces pushing in one direction and other, counterbalancing forces that restrain movement. The level of productivity in an organization may appear static, but sometimes it is being pushed higher — by the force of supervisory pressure, for example — and sometimes it is being restrained or even decreased by a counterforce, such as a norm of the work group. There are many different counterbalancing forces in any given situation, and what is called a force-field analysis is used to identify the two sets of forces.

Change from the status quo is therefore a two-step process. First, a force-field analysis is conducted, and then the intensity of a force or set of forces is either increased or decreased. Change can be fostered by adding to or increasing the intensity of the forces Lewin labeled *driving forces* — that is, forces that push in the desired direction for change. Or change can be fostered by diminishing the opposing or restraining forces. Lewin's theory predicts that the better of these two choices is to reduce the intensity of the restraining forces. By adding forces or increasing the intensity on the driving side, a simultaneous increase would occur on the restraining side, and the overall tension for the system — whether it is a person, a group, or an organization — would intensify. The better choice, then, is to reduce the restraining forces.

This facet of Lewin's field theory helps us to determine not only the nature of change but how to accomplish it more effectively. Lewinian theory argues that it is more efficacious to direct change at the group level than at the individual level.

If one attempts to change an attitude or the behavior of an individual without attempting to change the same behavior or attitude in the group to which the individual belongs, then the individual will be a deviate and either will come under pressure from the group to get back into line or will be rejected entirely. Thus, the major leverage point for change is at the group level — for example, by modifying a group norm or standard. According to Lewin (1958):

> As long as group standards are unchanged, the individual will resist change more strongly the farther he is to depart from group standards. If the group standard itself is changed, the resistance which is due to the relation between individual and group standard is eliminated. (p. 210)

Adherence to Lewinian theory from the standpoint of application involves viewing the organization as a social system, with many and varied subsystems, primarily groups. We look at the behavior of people in the organization in terms of 1) whether their needs jibe with the organization's directions, usually determined by their degree of commitment; 2) the norms to which people conform and the degree of that conformity; 3) how power is exercised (induced versus own forces); and 4) the decision-making process (involvement leading to commitment).

Changing Values Through the Group — Argyris

It is not possible to place the work of Chris Argyris in one category, one theory, or one conceptual framework. He has developed a number of minitheories whose relationship and possible overlap are not always apparent. He has always focused largely on interpersonal and group behavior, however, and he has emphasized behavioral change within a group context, along the same value lines as McGregor's (1960) Theory Y. The work described in *Management and Organizational Development: The Path from XA to YB* (Argyris, 1971) best illustrates this emphasis. Since Argyris has made many theoretical contributions, we shall briefly cover his work chronologically.

Argyris's early work (1962) may be characterized as emphasizing the relationship of individual personality and organizational dynamics. His objective was to look for ways in which this relationship could be "satisficed," with the person and the organization both compromising so that each could profit from each other. *Satisficed* is a word formed by combining *satisfied* and *suffice* and it means that there is an improvement but that it is less than optimal for each party. Although the relationship may never be optimal for both parties, it could still be better for both. For this relationship between the individual and the organization to be achieved, the organization must adjust its value system toward helping its members to be more psychologically healthy, less dependent on and controlled by the organization. The individuals must become more open with their feelings, more willing to trust one another, and more internally committed to the organization's goals.

In his thinking, research, and writing during the late 1960s and early 1970s, Argyris became more clearly associated with organization development. His thrust of this period was in 1) theorizing about competent consultation, and especially about the nature of an effective intervention, and 2) operationalizing organizational change in behavioral terms by McGregor's Theory Y. Regarding the first aspect, Argyris (1970) contends that, for any intervention into an organization-social system to be effective, it must generate valid information, lead to free, informed choice on the part of the client, and provide internal commitment by the client to the choices taken. More on this aspect of Argyris's work is provided in Chapter 5. For the second aspect, Argyris connects behaviors (he calls them Pattern A) with McGregor's Theory X and Theory Y (Pattern B). Argyris specifies the behavioral manifestations of someone who holds either of the sets of assumptions about human beings in organizations that were postulated earlier by McGregor (1960). Pattern A behaviors are characterized as predominantly intellectual rather than emotional, conforming rather than experimenting, individually oriented rather than group oriented, involving closer rather than open communications, and generally mistrusting rather than trusting. This pattern is the opposite of interpersonally competent behavior. Thus, Pattern B is an extension of Argyris's earlier facets of interpersonal competence.

More recently, Argyris has turned his attention to the gaps in people's behavior between what they say (he calls it espoused theory) and what they do (theory in action). People may say that they believe that McGregor's Theory Y assumptions about human beings are valid, for example, but they may act according to Pattern A. Argyris goes on to argue that as people become more aware of these gaps between their stated beliefs and their behavior, they will be more motivated to reduce the differences, to be more consistent. In one project Argyris tape-recorded managerial staff meetings, analyzed the recorded behaviors, and then showed the managers where their actions were not consistent with their words (Argyris, 1973). More recently, in collaboration with Don Schön, Argyris studied and elaborated the learning process involved in obtaining greater self-awareness and organizational awareness about human effectiveness (Argyris and Schön, 1978). Argyris and Schön argue that most organizations accomplish no more than "single-loop learning," that problems are solved or fixed and a single loop of learning is accomplished. For significant organizational improvement and for ensuring long-term survival and renewal, however, change must occur in more fundamental ways. Although problems must be solved in a single loop, new ways of learning how to solve problems must be learned as well. Another loop is thus added to the learning cycle, what Argyris and Schön refer to as "double-loop learning." Single-loop learning is like adjusting a thermostat to a standard that has already been established, whereas double-loop learning means confronting the current standard and creating a new one. This process of learning is analogous to if not the same as the way OD is sometimes defined as a planned process of change in the organization's culture — how we do things and how we relate to one another.

The Group Unconscious — Bion

Most people believe that everyone has an unconscious. Freud has clearly had an effect. Wilfred Bion believes, as others do, that there is also a group unconscious — a collective unconscious that is more than the sum of the individual unconsciouses — and he gives compelling but complex arguments (Bion, 1961; Rioch, 1970).

Bion believes that every group is actually composed of two groups, the work group and the basic-assumption group; that is, every group behaves as if it were two groups, one concerned with group accomplishment and rational actions, the other concerned with activity that stems from the unconscious and is irrational. Bion does not mean simply that a group is both rational and irrational. He goes far beyond this commonly accepted dichotomy.

The *work group* is the aspect of group functioning that is concerned with accomplishing what the group is composed to do, the task at hand. The work group is aware of its purpose, or at the outset knows that its initial task is to establish clarity of purpose. The work group is sure about, or quickly becomes sure about, roles and responsibilities in the group. The work group is also clearly conscious of the passage of time and the procedures and processes needed to accomplish the task.

How many times have you been a member or leader of a group that fit such a description? I suspect that it has not been very often, if ever. Bion states that groups do not behave in this clearly rational and sensible way because there is always another group operating simultaneously — the *basic-assumption* group.

Bion theorizes that all groups function according to basic assumptions, that groups operate as if certain things are inevitable. Perhaps an analogy will help to explain. In the early days of automobiles, many people made the basic assumption that no motorized vehicle could go faster than a horse, and these people acted accordingly. In fact, some of them eventually lost money because they bet heavily on that assumption. The point is that they acted as if their belief were true and inevitable.

According to Bion, basic-assumption groups may take, at least predominantly, one of three forms: the dependency group, the fight-flight group, and the pairing group. The *dependency group* assumes that the reason the group exists is to be protected and to be assured of providence by its leader. The group members act immaturely, childishly, and as if they know little or nothing as compared with the leader. The leader is all powerful and wise. In the dependency group, the leader is typically idolized. We mortals are neither omnipotent nor omniscient, however, and the group members soon realize that they must seek a "new messiah." The cycle then repeats itself with a new leader.

The *fight-flight* group assumes that is must preserve itself, that its survival is at stake, so group members act accordingly. Taking action is the key to survival, as in the proverbial army command: "Do something even if it's wrong!" It is the *group* that must be preserved, so individuals may be sacrificed through fight or abandonment (flight). The leader's role in this basic-assumption group is clear: to lead the group into battle or retreat. The best leader is one who acts in a paranoid manner, assuming, "They're out to get us, gang!" Eventually and inevitably the leader will not meet all the group's demands, at which point the group panics and searches for a new leader.

In the *pairing* group the assumption is that the group's purpose is to give birth to a new messiah. The leader in this case is purely incidental, and the group must quickly get on with the business of bringing forth the new savior. Two members therefore pair off to procreate. The two may be both male, both female, or male and female, but the basic assumption is that when two people pair, the pairing is sexual in nature, even though it takes the innocent form of establishing a subcommittee. Although new life and hope may be provided, the new messiah, as the Christian

Messiah, will soon be done away with. All the basic-assumption groups behave as if the leader must be replaced or, to use Bion's more dramatic and graphic terminology, as if the leader must be crucified.

Although the work group and the basic-assumption group are functioning simultaneously, their degree of activity varies. At times the work group is predominant and at other times the basic-assumption group holds sway.

Bion was never an OD practitioner; he was a psychotherapist. His theory, however, is applicable to interventions with teams, consultations with leaders, and diagnoses of possible processes of collusion. For a direct application and extension of the latter group or organizational dynamic, see Harvey's "Abilene Paradox" (1974), an extension of Bion's theory that explains collusive behavior on the part of members of a group.

For the OD practitioner serving as a consultant to an organizational team, Bion's theory is particularly useful for diagnosing internal problems, especially those concerning team members' relationships with the leader. For example, when subordinates defer to the boss for most if not all decisions, a basic-assumption mode of dependency may be occurring, with the work group mode being submerged. Calling this process to the attention of the group may break the basic-assumption mode and help to facilitate the group's task accomplishment. An OD practitioner might intervene with a comment like, "We seem to be looking to (the boss) for practically all of our problem solutions," and follow up with a question such as, "Don't we have experience among us that we could tap into more?" Helping a work group to stay focused on its task is a way of preventing flight and another example of how to apply Bion's theory.

Total System Perspective

Participative Management, The One Best Way — Likert

Likert is best known for two concepts: the *linking pin* notion of management and the four-system model of organizations. He is also known for his unequivocal advocacy of participative management as the approach to be taken by managers, regardless of organizational type. Likert's method for organization development is survey feedback. We shall consider each of these concepts briefly.

Likert's (1961) idea of the linking pin originated from his desire to design organizations in a more decentralized form without eliminating the hierarchical structure. He also wanted to incorporate more opportunity for group activity, especially group decision making, in the managerial process. Thus, each manager is simultaneously a member of two groups, one in which he or she manages and is the leader and one in which he or she is a subordinate and follows the leadership of a boss. By being a member of both these hierarchical groups, the person becomes a key link within the vertical chain of command. This linkage manifests itself primarily in activities involving communication and resolution of conflict. The manager-subordinate, therefore, is the primary conduit for information and facilitates the resolution of conflict, by virtue of the linking position, when there are differences between the two vertically connected organizational groups. An organization chart is drawn so that groups overlap vertically rather than in the more traditional way, as separate boxes connected only by lines.

Likert (1967) has described four major models or systems of organization design: the *autocratic*, the *benevolent autocratic*, the *consultative*, and the *participative*. He uses seven organizational functions to describe the four models differentially: *leadership*, *motivation*, *communication*, *interaction and influence*, *decision making*, *goal setting*, and *control*. His "Profile of Organizational Characteristics," a diagnostic questionnaire, is organized according to these seven functions and four models. Organization members' answers to the questionnaire provide a perceptual profile of the organization. The profile is derived from the respondents' views of how the seven functions are managed and depicts which of the four systems seems to be predominant, at least in the eyes of the respondents.

Likert not only argues that there is one best way to manage, he also espouses one best way to conduct an organization development effort. His method is survey feedback, the survey instrument being his Profile of Organizational Characteristics and the feedback being organized and analyzed according to the four-system model of organizational management. In an organization development effort, then, Likert's approach is highly data-based, but the diagnosis is largely limited to the functions he deems important. Once the survey data are collected, they are given back in profile form to organizational family units — to a boss and his or her team. This group then considers the data in light of their particular situation and organizational mandate, then decides on a plan for changes they want to make, and finally takes the necessary action for implementing the plan. Approximately a year later, the organization should take another survey to check progress and to plan and implement further changes.

Although organizational change agents may be uncomfortable with Likert's one best way and may prefer an approach that is more contingent and perhaps more flexible, they can be very sure of the direction and the objectives of the change effort.

It All Depends — Lawrence and Lorsch

For an organization to operate efficiently and effectively, one person cannot do everything, and every organizational member cannot do the same thing. In any organization, therefore, there is a division of labor. Lawrence and Lorsch (1967, 1969) call this differentiation. In an organization with many divisions, some people must provide coordination, so that what the organization does is organized in some fashion. Lawrence and Lorsch label this process integration. Their approach is sometimes referred to as a theory of differentiation-integration. A more appropriate label, however, and the one they prefer, is *contingency theory*. They believe that how an organization should be structured and how it should be managed depend on several factors, primarily the organization's environment, or its marketplace. The central elements of the Lawrence and Lorsch contingency theory are differentiation, integration, the organization–environment interface, and the implicit contract between the employees and management.

Differentiation means dividing up tasks so that everything that needs to be done is accomplished. To determine the degree of differentiation in an organization, Lawrence and Lorsch consider four variables:

1. *Goal certainty.* Are goals clear and easily measured or ambiguous and largely qualitative?
2. *Structure.* Is the structure formal, with precise policy and procedures, or loose and flexible, with policy largely a function of current demand?
3. *Interaction.* Is there considerable interpersonal and intergroup communication and cooperation or very little?
4. *Timespan of feedback.* Do people in the organization see the results of their work quickly or does it take a long time?

The more that units within an organization differ from one another along these four dimensions, the more differentially structured the organization is. Some units may be very sure of their goals while others are not so sure, and some units may follow strict and precise work procedures while other units are still trying to formulate working procedures. It should be clear, therefore, that highly differentiated organizations are more difficult to coordinate. In a pyramidal organization, the coordination and the resolution of conflict are handled by the next higher level of management. When organizations are simultaneously highly differentiated and decentralized with respect to management, Lawrence and Lorsch argue that integrator roles are needed, that certain people must be given specific assignments for coordinating and integrating diverse functions. These people may or may not be in key decision-making positions, but they ensure that decisions are made by someone or by the appropriate group.

Should an organization be structured in centralized (pyramidal) or decentralized fashion? We already know the answer: It depends. But on *what* does it depend? Lawrence and Lorsch state that it depends primarily on the organization's environment, on whether the environment is complex and rapidly changing, as in the electronics industry, or relatively simple (one or two major markets) and stable (raw materials forthcoming and predictable and market likely to remain essentially the same in the foreseeable future). The more complex the environment, the more decentralized and flexible management should be. Lawrence and Lorsch's reasoning is that, the more rapidly changing the environment, the more necessary it is that the organization have people monitoring these changes, and the more they should be in a position to make decisions on the spot. When the organization's environment is not particularly complex and when conditions are relatively stable, management should be more centralized, since this way of structuring is more efficient.

Lawrence and Lorsch consider matters of conflict resolution because conflicts arise quickly and naturally in a highly differentiated organization and the management of these conflicts is critical for efficient and effective organizational functioning. Moreover, if the organization is highly differentiated and decentralized, conflict is even more likely.

Finally, how well an organization operates is also a function of the nature of the interface between management and employees. Lawrence and Lorsch recognize the importance of individual motivation and effective supervision. They tend to view motivation in terms of expectancy, believing that employees' motivation (and morale) is based on the degree to which their expectations about how they should be treated are actually met by management in the work environment.

In summary, Lawrence and Lorsch are known as contingency theorists. They advocate no single form of organizational structure or single style of management. The structure and the style depend on the business of the organization and its environment — how variable or how stable it is.

Lawrence and Lorsch have been among the most influential theorists for OD practitioners. There is something appealing about the idea of considering contingencies before acting.

The Organization as a Family — Levinson

Harry Levinson believes that an organization can be psychoanalyzed and that an organization operates like a family, with the chief executive officer as the father. According to Levinson, all organizations "recapitulate the basic family structure in a culture." Thus, the type of organization Levinson understands best, of course, is the family-owned business, and his theory about organizations and how they operate and change has its roots in Freudian psychology (Levinson, 1972a, b).

Levinson does not look at organizations exclusively through psychoanalytical glasses, however. He is well aware that structure, the type of business, and the outside environment affect the internal behavioral dynamics of organizations. More important for Levinson's diagnosis of an organization, however, is the nature of the organization's personality (we might call it culture). He believes that an organization has a personality, just as an individual does, and that the health of an organization, like that of a person, can be determined in terms of how effectively the various parts of the personality are integrated. He refers to this process as *maintaining equilibrium*. Levinson also believes that implicit psychological contracts exist between management and employees, based on earlier experiences from family life. If the employees behave themselves (are good boys and girls), the parents (management) will reward them appropriately. Thus, the psychological contract is characterized by dependency. Note that this aspect of Levinson's theory is similar to Argyris's theory.

Continuing the psychoanalytic paradigm, Levinson theorizes that the chief executive officer represents the ego ideal for the organizational family and that this ideal, for better or for worse, motivates the kinds of people who are attracted to the organization in the first place, the interaction patterns among people in the organization, especially in matters of authority, and the kinds of people who are promoted. If a chief executive officer stays in office for a long time, the personality of the organization slowly crystallizes over the years; those who aspire to the ego ideal stay in the organization, and those who do not, leave. Accordingly, Levinson believes that history is a critical factor in diagnosing an organization.

Levinson is a clinical psychologist who became more interested in organizational health than in individual psychodynamics as a result of his work at the Menninger Clinic. He has applied the principles of individual clinical therapy to his consulting practice with organizations. His approach as a consultant is 1) to immerse himself as deeply as possible in the psychodynamics of the organization; 2) to take a thorough history of the organization, just as a clinician would in the initial session with a patient; 3) to work predominantly with top management, since they tend to shape the personality of the organization and are therefore in the best position to change it; and 4) to pay particular attention to the stress factors in the organization and to how organizational members cope. In regard to this last point, Levinson is considered the "great worrier" among OD theorists. He worries about executive stress (Levinson, 1975) and about the incidence in an organization of such variables as psychosomatic illnesses, absenteeism, and business pressures, such as the all-out emphasis many organizations place on meeting the "bottom line." Levinson is very interested in what people do with their energy, in whether human energy in the organization is directed toward goal accomplishment or toward coping with stress.

In summary, as a consultant, Levinson uses the clinical case method in diagnosis, intervenes primarily at the top of an organization, and bases his theory on psychoanalysis. In his own words:

> You've got to take into account all the factors in an organization, just as you gather all the main facts of a person's life in taking a case history. But you need a comprehensive theory like psychoanalysis to make sense of all the facts, to make it hang together in a useful way. (1972a: p. 126)

Summary

At the risk of oversimplification, I have summarized ten theorists' views by categorizing them according to their perspectives and emphases and according to potential applications of their theoretical approaches. A summary of these factors is given in Table 3–1. Keep in mind that there is no single, all-encompassing theory for organization development. What we have are several minitheories that help us understand certain aspects of organizational behavior and OD. Taken together and comparatively, they become more useful to the practitioner who must cope with an ever-changing, complex, total organization.

Thus, organization development comes from many sources and has its roots in more than one methodology and in a variety of theories and concepts. The background provided in this chap-

see p. 53

Table 3-1
Summary of Primary OD Theorists According to Their Perspectives, Emphases, and Applications

Perspective	Theorist	Emphasis	Application
Individual	Maslow and Herzberg	Individual needs	Career development, job enrichment
	Vroom and Lawler	Individual expectancies and values	Reward system design, performance appraisal
	Hackman and Oldham	Job satisfaction	Job and work design, job enrichment
	Skinner	Individual performance	Incentive systems, reward system design
Group	Lewin	Norms and values	Changing conformity patterns
	Argyris	Interpersonal competence and values	Training and education
	Bion	Group unconscious, psychoanalytic basis	Group behavior diagnosis
System	Likert	Management style and approach	Change to participative management
	Lawrence and Lorsch	Organizational structure	Change contingent on organizational environment
	Levinson	Organization as a family, psychoanalytic basis	Diagnosis of organization according to familial patterns

ter, though varied, nevertheless has commonality. The trunk from these roots might be expressed as the attempt to improve an organization with methods that involve people and to create conditions whereby the talents of these people are used more effectively.

4

Organization Development as a Process of Change

Recall the definition of OD: a planned process of change in an organization's culture through the utilization of behavioral science technology and theory. The focus of this chapter is on the "process of change" and "utilization of . . . theory."

Although the practice of organization development may be based on portions of several theories from the behavioral sciences, as shown in the previous chapter, there is no single, all-encompassing theory of OD. This no doubt constitutes a weakness of the field, but it is not surprising, since OD is very young as a field, having its origins around 1960, and is based on several disciplines. Nevertheless, most practitioners agree that three models are the underlying and guiding frames of reference for any OD effort: 1) the action research model; 2) Lewin's three-step model of system change — unfreezing, moving, and refreezing; and 3) phases of planned change as delineated by Lippitt, Watson, and Westley (1958). The three models are not mutually exclusive, and all stem from the original thinking of Kurt Lewin.

Action Research

In practice, the words *action research* are reversed (Brown, 1972), for initially research is first conducted and then action is taken as a direct result of what the research data are interpreted to indicate. As French and Bell (1978) have pointed out, action research came from two independent sources, one a person of action, John Collier, who was commissioner of Indian Affairs from 1933 to 1945, the other a person of research, Kurt Lewin. Collier worked to bring about change in ethnic relations and was a strong advocate of conducting research to determine the "central areas of needed action" (Collier, 1945). He labeled this kind of research "action research."

Although Lewin was an academician — a scholar, theoretician, and researcher — he was just as eminent a man of action (Marrow, 1969). Moreover, he pulled it all together when he stated that there is "no action without research, and no research without action" (Lewin, 1946). Lewin and his colleagues and students conducted many action research projects in several different domains: community and racial relations, leadership, eating habits, and intergroup conflict. The action research project that is perhaps most relevant to OD was conducted by John P. R. French (a student of Lewin's and now a professor at the University of Michigan) and his client, Lester Coch. Their famous study of workers' resistance to change in a pajama factory not only illustrated action research at its best but provided the theoretical basis for what we now call participative management (Coch and French, 1948).

Wendell French (1969), Frohman, Sashkin, and Kavanagh (1976), and Schein (1980) have taken the action research model and made it directly applicable and relevant to the organization development process. Figure 4–1 shows French's adaptation.

Lewin's Three-Step Procedure of Change

According to Lewin (1958), the first step in the process of change is *unfreezing* the present level of behavior. To reduce prejudice, for example, the unfreezing step might be catharsis (All-

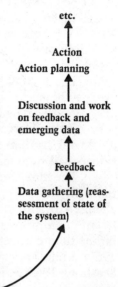

etc.

Action (new behavior)

Action planning (determination of objectives and how to get there)

Discussion and work on data by client group (new attitudes, new perspectives emerge)

Feedback to client group (e.g., in team-building sessions, summary feedback by consultant; elaboration by group)

Data gathering

Action

Action planning

Discussion and work on feedback and emerging data

Feedback

Data gathering (reassessment of state of the system)

Joint action planning (objectives of OD program and means of attaining goals, e.g., team-building)

Feedback to key client or client group

Further data gathering

Data gathering and diagnosis by consultant

Consultation with behavioral scientist consultant

Key executive perception of problems

Figure 4–1
Action-Research Model for Organization Development

Source: W. L. French, "Organization Development: Objectives, Assumptions, and Strategies," © 1969 by the Regents of the University of California. Reprinted from *California Management Review*, Volume XII, No. 2, p. 26 by permission of The Regents.

port, 1945) or participation in a series of sensitivity training sessions (Rubin, 1967). For organizational change, the unfreezing step might be a series of management training sessions in which the objective for change was a more participative approach (Blake, Mouton, Barnes, and Greiner, 1964; Shepard, 1960) or data feedback from a survey that showed serious problems in the managerial process of the organization (Bowers, 1973; Nadler, 1977).

The second step, *movement,* is to take action that will change the social system from its original level of behavior or operation to a new level. This action could be organization structuring (Foltz, Harvey, and McLaughlin, 1974), team development (Beckhard and Lake, 1971), or any number of what OD practitioners call interventions.

The *refreezing* step involves the establishment of a process that will make the new level of behavior "relatively secure against change" (Lewin, 1958). This refreezing process may include different conforming patterns, or new forms, such as collaboration rather than competition (Davis, 1967; Tannenbaum and Davis, 1969), a new approach to managing people (Marrow, Bowers, and Seashore, 1967; Seashore and Bowers, 1970), or a new reward system that will positively reinforce the desired behavior change (Lawler, 1977).

Thus, according to Lewin, bringing about lasting change means initially unlocking or unfreezing the present social system. This might require some kind of confrontation (Beckhard, 1967) or a process of reeducation. Next, behavioral movement must occur in the direction of desired change, such as a reorganization. Finally, deliberate steps must be taken to ensure that the new state of behavior remains relatively permanent. These three steps are simple to state but not simple to implement. Lippitt, Watson, and Westley (1958) and Schein and Bennis (1965: see especially ch. 10) have helped to clarify these steps by elaborating on them.

Phases of Planned Change

The Lippitt, Watson, and Westley (1958) model of planned change expands Lewin's three steps to five phases. They use the world *phase* deliberately, since *step* connotes a discrete action or event rather than the more likely reality, that Step 1 has probably not been completed when Step 2 is being taken, and so forth. Their five phases are

1. Development of a need for change (Lewin's unfreezing)
2. Establishment of a change relationship
3. Working toward change (moving)
4. Generalization and stabilization of change (refreezing)
5. Achieving a terminal relationship

Lippitt, Watson, and Westley viewed the change process from the perspective of the change agent. Their concept of change agent is a professional, typically a behavioral scientist, who is external or internal to the organization involved in the change process. In OD terms, this person is the OD practitioner or consultant. Lippitt and his colleagues go on to state:

> The decision to make a change may be made by the system itself, after experiencing pain (malfunctioning) or discovering the possibility of improvement, or by an outside change agent who observes the need for change in a particular system and takes the initiative in establishing a helping relationship with that system. (Lippitt, Watson, and Westley, 1958: p. 10)

With respect to Phase 1 — the development of a need for change — Lippitt, Watson, and Westley suggest that the unfreezing occurs in one of three ways: 1) a change agent demonstrates the need by, for example, presenting data from interviews that indicate a serious problem exists; 2) a third party sees a need and brings the change agent and the potential client system together; or 3) the client system becomes aware of its own need and seeks consultative help.

By establishment of a change relationship, Phase 2, the authors mean the development of a collaborative working effort between the change agent and the client system. Lippitt and his colleagues make an important point when they note that "often the client system seems to be seeking assurance that the potential change agent is different enough from the client system to be a real expert and yet enough like it to be thoroughly understandable and approachable" (p. 134). Striking this balance is critical to effective consultation in organization development.

Most of their elaboration on Lewin's three steps is in the moving phase, or, as Lippitt and his colleagues call it, working toward change. There are three subphases to this third major phase:

1. *Clarification* or diagnosis of the client system's problem, which consists primarily of the change agent's collecting information and attempting to understand the system, particularly the problem areas.
2. *Examination* of alternative routes and goals, which involves establishing goals and intentions of action and also includes determining the degree of motivation for change and the beginning of a process of focusing energy.
3. *Transformation* of intentions into actual change efforts, which is the *doing* part — implementing a new organization structure, conducting a specific training program, installing a new record system, and the like.

Refreezing, or the generalization and stabilization of change, is the fourth major phase. The key activity in this phase is spreading the change to other parts of the total system. This phase also includes the establishment of mechanisms or activities that will maintain the momentum that was gathered during the previous phases. Lippitt and his colleagues call this a process of institutionalization. Hornstein et al. (1971) view this institutionalization process in two ways: as normative support for the change and as structural support for the change. By normative support they mean that, in the refreezing phase, organization members are conforming to new norms. To ensure this form of institutionalization, organization members must be involved in the planning and implementing of the action steps for change. Involvement leads to commitment — in this case, commitment to new norms. Structural support may take the form of new organizational arrangements — that is, new reporting and accountability relationships, as reflected in a new organization chart — or the placement of guardians of the new culture, the new conforming patterns. These guardians, or facilitators, of the new culture are people whose job it is 1) to monitor the state of the organization's effectiveness, 2) to see that the information that is monitored is reported to the appropriate people in the organization, 3) to provide help in understanding the information, especially in the diagnosis of problems, 4) to assist in the planning and implementation of action steps for further changes, and 5) to provide additional expertise in helping the organization to continue to change and renew where appropriate. Their primary responsibility, therefore, is to help regulate change as an organizational way of life. Hornstein and his colleagues go on to state:

> Initially, this role is typically fulfilled by an outside consultant to the organization. Frequently, he attempts to work in conjunction with some person (or persons) inside the organization. If the internal person is not trained in OD, the external consultant will usually encourage the internal person(s) and other key individuals in the organization to develop their own resources in this area. (Hornstein et al., 1971: p. 352)

In other words, the more the consultant can arrange for OD-trained people to be permanent organization members, the more likely it is that the initiated change will last and become institutionalized as a way of life.

For the final phase, Lippitt and his colleagues argue for the achievement of a terminal relationship. What they mean is that the relationship between the change agent and the client must end. They contend that it is common for clients to become dependent on change agents and that change agents' ultimate goal is to work themselves out of a job. The underlying value of this model for change is that it creates within the client system the expertise to solve its own problems in the future, at least those problems that fall within the same universe as the original change problem.

The Generic Model for Organizational Change

The three models covered so far in this chapter — action research; Lewin's three steps of unfreezing, moving, and refreezing; and Lippitt, Watson, and Westley's five phases of planned change — are all part of a generic model for bringing about organizational change. This is not accidental, of course, since all three models are based on the original thinking of Kurt Lewin.

The generic model might be described as a process by which a consultant collects information about the nature of an organization (the research) and then helps the organization to change by way of a sequence of phases that involve those who are directly affected, the organization members themselves. This more general model consists of the following elements:

1. An outside consultant or change agent
2. The gathering of information (data) from the client system by the consultant for purposes of understanding more about the inherent nature of the system, determining major domains in need of change (problems), and reporting this information back to the client system so that appropriate action can be taken
3. Collaborative planning between the consultant and the client system for purposes of change (action)
4. Implementation of the planned change, which is based on valid information (data) and is conducted by the client system, with the continuing help of the consultant
5. Institutionalization of the change

In an attempt to summarize and integrate the three models of change that we have considered thus far, Figure 4–2 compares Lewin's (1958) three steps, the action research model provided by French (1969) and Schein (1980), and Lippitt, Watson, and Westley's (1958) phases of planned change. Note that the action research model for OD is the main reference point for comparison.

Earlier thinking about planned change, especially Lippitt et al. (1958) emphasized the role of the change agent as data collector, data interpreter, and feedback provider. The change agent was depicted as doing practically everything. Current practice of OD emphasizes the role of the practitioner more in terms of *facilitation*, helping the client to do many of these activities themselves. Organizational development consulting tends to be unique

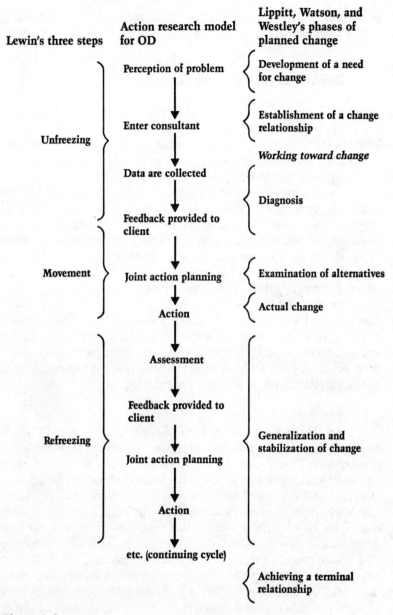

Lewin's three steps	Action research model for OD	Lippitt, Watson, and Westley's phases of planned change
	Perception of problem	Development of a need for change
Unfreezing	Enter consultant	Establishment of a change relationship
	Data are collected	*Working toward change*
	Feedback provided to client	Diagnosis
Movement	Joint action planning	Examination of alternatives
	Action	Actual change
	Assessment	
	Feedback provided to client	
Refreezing	Joint action planning	Generalization and stabilization of change
	Action	
	etc. (continuing cycle)	
		Achieving a terminal relationship

Figure 4–2
Summary Comparison of the Three Models of Change

in this regard, in any case distinct from management consulting, where the consultant usually does all of this work for the client.

Practicing OD: A Case History

The action research model and the phases of planned change provide the framework for OD practice. We shall consider in more specificity these practice phases, but first let us consider an actual case of OD consultation that should help our later understanding of the more specific practice phases.

I was contacted initially by Carol, the manager of human resources for a regional division of a large, international financial corporation. She reported directly to Ron, the regional manager. Carol called me because I had previously consulted with other divisions of the corporation and was therefore familiar with the firm's business. She also told me that she had sought advice from others in the corporation and that I had been recommended. She further explained that Ron was new in his position as regional manager and was anxious to make some changes. He was considering an off-site meeting with his senior management group and believed that an outside consultant might be helpful. Carol then asked if I would be interested and, if so, if we could have lunch together soon to explore the matter.

Exploration

At the lunch meeting a few days later, Carol and I asked one another many questions. She was interested in what I had done before, how I liked to work, what I might do or suggest if such-and-such were to happen, what I knew about her company's business, and whether I would be interested in continuing to consult with them if the initial effort went well. I asked her such questions as why the business had been losing money for four years in a row; what Ron's predecessor was like; what Ron was like (his managerial style, his previous job history, how people in the region, especially the senior management group, felt about him, and whether any of the others thought they should have become the new regional manager instead of Ron); how the senior management group worked together — whether off-site meetings were common occurrences; and so forth. Toward the end of our exploratory discussion, Carol explained that she needed to talk further with Ron and that she would be in touch with me again soon.

Meeting with Ron

The following week Carol called and scheduled a meeting for me with Ron. In my meeting with Ron, it was soon clear to me that he trusted Carol a great deal. He was essentially sold on me, and all we needed to do was to discuss details. He explained that, although he had been in the region for more than three years, as head of consumer services, he had only been regional manager for a month. He felt pressure from higher management to make the region profitable, and he reasoned that he must have his senior management group solidly with him in order to "turn the region around." He further stated that he wanted to have an off-site meeting with his senior management group to establish two-year profit goals, to develop an overall regional business strategy, and to begin the process of building a senior management *team*.

For my part, I explained that I would like to conduct individual interviews with the members of his senior management group, including himself, determine if they thought an off-site meeting was appropriate (we would not have the meeting if enough of them said no), summarize and analyze the information from the interviews, meet with him again to go over the data, plan the meeting (if warranted), and clarify our respective roles. He would lead the meeting and I would help; in OD language, my role would be a *facilitating* one.

Agreement

We reached agreement concerning what Ron wanted and how I wanted to proceed. This verbal agreement was followed a few days later with an exchange of letters to confirm our agreement in writing.

Interviews

Over a one-week period, I conducted one-hour interviews with each member of the senior management group. This group is depicted in the chart shown in Fig. 4–3.

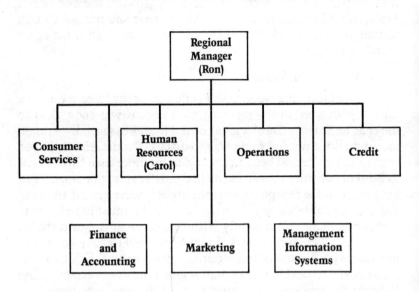

Figure 4–3
Organization Chart for Regional Division of International Financial Corporation

I explained to each manager that the interview would be confidential and that only a summary of the interviews in aggregate form would become public. Although I asked many questions in each interview, I asked four general questions of everyone:

1. What are the strengths of the region?
2. What are the weaknesses of the region?
3. Are you in favor of the off-site meeting?
4. What should be the objectives of the off-site meeting?

The interviews went well. All the managers were cooperative and expressed themselves openly and candidly, and I took many notes.

Summary and Analysis of Interviews

Although some of the managers thought the off-site meeting was somewhat premature because Ron had been in his position only for one month, others believed that the timing was right. Regardless of the timing, however, all thought that an off-site meeting was a good idea. Thus, the summary of my interviews was categorized according to the three other questions: strengths and weaknesses of the region and objectives of the off-site meeting. Table 4–1 provides a partial listing of some of the major points of the interviews. As is typical for such an activity, the weaknesses listed outnumbered the strengths. People, especially managers, tend to focus more on problems than on what is going well or is positive for the organization.

Some general problems in the region became clear to me as a result of the interviews. Although the group believed that they were highly knowledgeable and experienced in their business, they recognized that continuing to make no profits was not going to get them where they wanted to go, especially in their individual careers. There was also a conflict over whether theirs was a marketing and sales organization or a consumer services organization. Actually, it had to be both, but, from the standpoint of strategy and with respect to individuals' roles and responsibilities in lower levels of management, there was considerable ambiguity. This ambiguity contributed to problems of priorities, numbers 2 and 3 in the list of weaknesses. The emphasis on structure and financial objectives was therefore appropriate in the major objectives for the off-site meeting.

Plan for the Off-site Meeting

Ron and I met before the off-site meeting to go over my summary and analysis of the interview information and to plan the meeting. I gave Ron the summary and analysis of the interviews just as I would later give it to the entire group. Thus, Ron received the same information but received it earlier. The purposes of this advance notice were, first, to use the information as a basis for planning an agenda for the meeting, and, second, to allow Ron to have time to understand and react to the information before the meeting. Ron would then have an opportunity to discuss his reactions to the information, particularly his feelings, so that if he felt defensive, for example, he could talk about it with me and not be as defensive during the meeting. In such situations, especially if it is the first time, bosses frequently receive more criticism for problems than do any other member of the group.

Table 4–1
Partial Summary of Eight Interviews Conducted with a Regional Senior Management Group

Strengths of the Region

1. Senior management group is highly experienced in the business (7)
2. Commitment of work force; community spirit (5)
3. Considerable opportunity; natural market area (3)
4. Good people throughout (3)
5. Last four years we have experienced success in many areas (3)
6. Have become more of a marketing organization (3)
7. We are technologically superior and a market leader as compared with our competitors (3)
8. Creativity (2)
9. Managers think entrepreneurially (2)

Weaknesses

1. Our marketing and services system (6)
2. Try to do too many things at once; do not establish priorities (3)
3. Region priorities are always secondary to individual manager's (3)
4. Lack of management depth (3)
5. Little planning (3)
6. Structure (2)
7. High costs (2)
8. Overly change-oriented (2)
9. Poor reward system (2)
10. Low morale (2)
11. Internal competition (2)
12. High degree of mistrust (2)

Objectives of Off-site Meeting

1. Agree on the regional structure (7)
2. Set financial objectives for next two years (6)
3. List of things we need to do and stop doing (4)
4. Must hear from Ron about his team notions, ideas, expectations (4)
5. Some ventilation of feelings needed (3)
6. Must come together more as a top management team (3)
7. Establish standards for performance (3)
8. Increase mutual respect (2)

Note: The number in parentheses after each item indicates the number of respondents who specifically mentioned that point. The total number of interviewees was 8.

Even if interview comments are not specifically directed at the bosses, they may feel responsible and accountable for the problems because of their positions, regardless of where the actual causes may lie. In Ron's case, he was not angry and he was not particularly defensive. He didn't think he had contributed to the weaknesses and problems any more than anyone else had. If he had been regional manager longer than a month, of course, his feelings may have been different. Ron was pleased with his group's openness and accuracy regarding the issues, and he was enthusiastic about the upcoming meeting.

Our plan for the meeting was simple and straightforward. We wanted as little interference and distraction as possible, so we would hold the meeting at a resort hotel that was fairly remote yet comfortable. The site was less than two hours away from the region's headquarters by automobile, and it met our criteria. Regarding the agenda, we planned to begin at 4 P.M. on Wednesday. Ron would open the meeting with a statement of his goals and expectations regarding the meeting, and I would follow with a summary of the interviews. The group would then have a chance to react to and discuss the interview summary. Before dinner Ron would present some financial data that would show clearly how the region compared with the other regions (they were close to the bottom), and after some discussion we would eat dinner together as a group. Thursday morning would be devoted to setting a two-year profit goal and to establishing priorities among the many objectives. Thursday afternoon we would discuss potential obstacles to reaching the profit goal and to realizing some of the more specific objectives of the region, such as clarifying their objectives regarding the balance of marketing versus service. Friday morning we would discuss an overall strategy that would incorporate the profit goal and these objectives, and Friday afternoon would be devoted to a summary of the meeting, to members' reactions to and critique of the meeting, and to a discussion of the specific plans for follow-up.

The Off-site Meeting

The meeting proceeded essentially as planned. We took a two-hour break for lunch and some physical recreation in the middle of the day on Thursday and then worked from 2 P.M. to about 7 P.M. On Friday we had a quick lunch and continued to work until about 3 P.M., when we adjourned. This was somewhat short for such a meeting, but adequate. During the summary and critique of the meeting, I also participated, giving my observations of them as a group, and making suggestions about how they could improve their work together as a team. Everyone considered the meeting to have been worthwhile and useful, and Ron was particularly pleased. He believed that the formation of a team, as opposed to an administrative aggregate of senior managers, had begun, and I agreed.

After the Off-site Meeting

A few weeks after the meeting, Ron and I met again and agreed on a plan for my continued consultation. Some of the changes I helped to make were 1) installation of a planning function reporting directly to Ron; 2) reorganization of the consumer services area, particularly regarding the functions of marketing and sales as they related to service (an off-site meeting with the head of consumer services and his management group was part of the planning for these changes); 3) modifications in the reward and performance-appraisal processes of the region (I worked with Carol in this area); and 4) development of the senior management group into more of a team. Eventually, though certainly not overnight, the profit picture for the region began to change, and they did indeed move from the red to the black.

Now that we have the case as an illustration of organization development consultation, let us reconsider the steps I took so that we can translate the activities into OD language and understand more thoroughly the concepts and principles of this kind of consultation.

Phases of OD Practice

Based on the Lewinian concepts of unfreezing, change, and refreezing and on Lippitt, Watson, and Westley's (1958) phases of planned change, but oriented more specifically to current OD practice, Kolb and Frohman (1970) give seven phases to be followed in an OD consultation: scouting, entry, diagnosis, planning, action, evaluation, and termination. I have modified their list by putting scouting and entry together, separating contracting and feedback into distinct phases, using intervention instead of action, and eliminating termination. What Kolb and Frohman call *scouting*, I call *entry*, and I consider *contracting* a more appropriate term for what they label *entry*. Our differences are simply in labels and emphasis; the overall process is the same, except for *termination*, which I will explain later. Thus, my seven phases are

1. Entry
2. Contracting
3. Diagnosis
4. Feedback
5. Planning change
6. Intervention
7. Evaluation

We shall consider each of these phases in turn, using the case example to illustrate the particular characteristics of OD consultation.

Entry

Contact between the consultant and client is what initiates the entry phase. This contact may result from either the client's calling the consultant for an exploratory discussion about the possibility of an OD effort, as in the case example, or from the consultant's suggesting to the client that such an effort might be worthwhile. For an external consultant, the contact is likely to result from the client's initiative. For an internal consultant, either mode may occur. Internal consultants, being employees, typically feel some commitment to their organizations, or it may be part of their job descriptions to call on managers in the organization and suggest preliminary steps that might lead to an OD effort. Internal consultants also may have experienced success with organization development in one subsystem and may wish to spread this effect further within the organization. Initiating contacts with clients therefore comes naturally for internal OD practitioners, and there is certainly more opportunity for informal contacts to occur — at lunch, at committee meetings, and so forth — when questions can be asked and suggestions explored.

After the contact, the consultant and the client begin the process of *exploring* with each other the possibilities of a working relationship. The client is usually assessing 1) whether he or she can relate well with the consultant, 2) whether the consultant's previous experience is applicable to the present situation, and 3) whether the consultant is competent and can be trusted.

My lunch meeting with Carol, the regional human resources manager, served as the beginning of the exploration process. I repeated the process with Ron, the regional manager, but this second round was rapid, since it had already been facilitated by Carol's previous meeting with and assessment of me.

During the exploration process, the consultant is assessing 1) whether he or she can relate well with the client, 2) the motivation and values of the client, 3) the client's readiness for change, 4) the extent of resources for supporting a change effort, and 5) potential leverage points for change (whether the client has the power to make decisions that will lead to change or whether higher authority must be sought). In my conversation with Ron, I became satisfied that he was motivated and ready for change, that he had the resources, and that he had the leverage — enough autonomy to take considerable action without getting approval from higher management.

There are additional criteria and ways of determining a client's readiness for change. Pfeiffer and Jones (1978), for example, have developed a useful fifteen-item checklist for such a determination. They urge the consultant to check, among others, such things as flexibility of top management, possible labor contract limitations (which could be crucial if job enrichment, for example, were a potential intervention), any previous experience the organization may have had with OD (or what some may have called OD, regardless of what the activities were), structural flexibility with respect to the organization's design, and the interpersonal skills of those who would be involved.

Contracting

Assuming that the mutual explorations of the consultant and the client in the entry phase progress satisfactorily, the next phase in the process is negotiating a contract. If the entry process has gone smoothly, the contracting phase is likely to be brief. The contract is essentially a statement of agreement that succinctly clarifies what the consultant agrees to do. If it is done thoroughly, the contract will also state what the client intends to do. The contract may be nothing more than a verbal agreement, with a handshake, perhaps, or it may be a formal document, with notarized signatures. Most often, the contract is considerably more informal than the latter extreme, typically involving an exchange of letters between the two parties.

Unlike other types of contracts, the OD contract states more about process than about contact. According to Weisbord (1973), it is

> an explicit exchange of expectations . . . which clarifies for consultant and client three critical areas:
> 1. What each expects to get from the relationship;
> 2. How much time each will invest, when, and at what cost;
> 3. The ground rules under which the parties will operate. (p. 1)

My contract with Ron was fairly straightforward. The letters that we exchanged simply confirmed in writing what we had agreed to in our meeting. The letters summarized what I would do and some of what he planned to do. The case as I described it was indeed the implementation of our contract.

In our meeting following the off-site meeting, Ron and I agreed on a further contract, which was also confirmed in writing in an exchange of letters between us.

It is a good practice in OD consultation to renew or renegotiate the contract periodically. In my consultation with Ron, the second contract was essentially an extension of the first, occurring about three months after the earlier one. The timing of the renewal or renegotiation is not as important as seeing that this phase is repeated periodically. It is also a good practice to have the agreement in writing. Although an exchange of letters may not necessarily constitute a legal document, the written word usually helps to avoid misunderstandings.

Diagnosis

There are two steps within the diagnostic phase: gathering information and analyzing it. Diagnosis has usually begun even at the entry phase — if the consultant is alert. How the client reacts to the possibility of change at the outset may tell a great deal not only about the client as an individual but also about the part of the organization's culture that he or she represents. Initially, therefore, information gathering is accomplished through the consultant's observations, intuitions, and feelings. Later, more systematic methods are used, such as structured interviews, questionnaires, and summaries of such organizational documents as performance records and task force reports. Once the data are collected, the consultant must then put all the varieties of information together, summarize all the information without losing critical pieces, and finally organize the information so that the client can easily understand it and be able to work with it so that appropriate action can be taken.

As you will see in the next chapter, there are several models to help the consultant with both steps of the diagnostic phase: knowing *what* information to seek and knowing *how* to analyze and interpret the information.

In my initial work with Ron and his management group, I relied on three methods of data gathering: interviews, my observations, and my reading of two documents, one concerning Ron's thinking about long-range planning and another that summarized the issues regarding the problem of marketing versus service orientation.

My diagnosis consisted of 1) summarizing the data according to the categories of the interview questions (see Table 4–1) and elaborating on what the interviewees had said and 2) drawing certain conclusions from the combination of my observations and some relationships I perceived in the interview results.

Feedback

How effectively the consultant has summarized and analyzed the diagnostic information will determine the success of the feedback phase to a significant extent. This phase consists of holding meetings with the client system, usually first with the boss alone and then with the entire group from whom the data were collected. The size of the group would determine the number of feedback sessions to be held. If the client system consisted of a manager and his or her immediate subordinates only, then two sessions would be required — one with the manager alone and the second with the entire group, including the manager. If more than these two levels of the overall managerial hierarchy were included (for example, four levels of management, involving thirty or more people), then as many as four or five feedback sessions may be necessary. A feedback session should allow for ample discussion and debate. A small group that does not involve multiple levels of management is best for such purposes.

A feedback session generally has three steps. First, the consultant provides a summary of the data collected and some preliminary analysis. Next, there is a general discussion in which questions of clarification are raised and answered. Finally, some time is devoted to interpretation. At this stage some changes may be made in the consultant's analysis and interpretation. Thus, the consultant works collaboratively with the client group to arrive at a final diagnosis that accurately describes the current state of the system.

In my work with Ron and his management team, I followed essentially the steps I have just outlined. The feedback phase consisted, first, of our discussion of the interview results early in the off-site meeting. Toward the end of the meeting, I provided additional feedback, which was a combination of my observations of the group as they worked together for two days and my further analysis of the interview data. I told them, for example, that I had observed that their competition with one another, a weakness some of them had identified, conformed to a particular norm. The norm seemed to say: "Let's see who among us can best identify and analyze our problems and weaknesses as a region." Everyone tackled every issue and problem, and it appeared that winning the game of "best analysis" was critical to all. My diagnosis, with which they agreed, was based in a social-psychological frame of reference and was particularly related to the concept of norm.

Planning Change

The planning phase sometimes becomes the second half of the feedback session, as happened with Ron and his team. Once the diagnosis was understood and deemed accurate, action steps were planned immediately. It has been noted that a good diagnosis determines the intervention. The only required planning may be the implementation steps: what to do. The more complex the diagnosis or the larger the client system, however, the more likely it is that the planning phase becomes a later event, following the feedback sessions. It may be best generally to allow some time to pass between feedback and planning — a few days, perhaps, but probably no more than a week. This passage of time might allow the feedback to sink in and would create an opportunity for more thought to be given to the planning process.

The purposes of this planning phase are, first, to generate alternative steps for responding correctively to the problems identified in the diagnosis and, second, to decide on the step or order of steps to take. The OD practitioner again works collaboratively with the client system during this phase, primarily by helping to generate and explore the consequences of alternative action steps. The final decision of what steps to take is the client's, not the consultant's.

Intervention

The intervention phase consists of the action taken. The possibilities are numerous, and the selected interventions should be a direct reflection of and response to the diagnosis. Some examples of interventions at the individual level are job redesign and enrichment, training and management development, changes in the quality of working life, management by objectives, and career development. At the group level, interventions might include team building, the installation of autonomous work groups, or starting quality control circles. Resolving intergroup conflict might be an intervention, as might changing such structural dimensions of the organization as reporting relationships, moving toward or away from decentralization of authority, modifying physical settings, or creating informal structures in the organization.

The interventions used in Ron's region were team building, process consultation, some minor structural changes, career development, and a change in the region's reward system to include a bonus plan for managers.

Whatever the intervention might be, the OD practitioner

continues to work with the client system to help make the intervention successful. As Kolb and Frohman (1970) point out: "the failure of most plans lies in the unanticipated consequences of the change effort" (p. 60). The OD consultant's job is to help the client anticipate and plan for the unanticipated consequences.

Evaluation

It is usually best for someone other than the consultant to conduct an evaluation of any OD effort. The consultant cannot be totally objective, and it is difficult to concentrate on what needs changing and on evaluating its success at the same time (Lewicki and Alderfer, 1973).

The mode of evaluation may range from clients saying that they are pleased with the outcome to a systematic research effort employing controls and multiple data analyses. A more objective and systematic evaluation is obviously better, at least for determining cause and effect. It is difficult to do a highly scientific evaluation of OD efforts. The main problem, of course, is control; it is almost impossible to have a proper control group for comparison. Furthermore, the client is usually more interested in taking action that will pay off than in objectively determining whether the action results were attributable to the OD intervention. What is important to the client is whether the action taken was successful according to the usual business standards of profits, reduction of costs, and higher performance in general; what caused the success is less important. This was essentially the case with Ron and his region, and so no formal evaluation was conducted. Evaluation did occur, however, as I periodically checked and asked for feedback, and the profit results, although they did not necessarily prove a cause-and-effect relationship, were sufficient evaluation in this case.

Regardless of its form or index, evaluation is very important because the process usually reinforces the change effort, and it is a primary way to learn about the consequences of our action.

In Chapter 6 we shall consider evaluation in more depth. It should be clear that some form of evaluation is a critical part in the OD process. Although the evaluative effort does not have to meet all the standards of rigorous research and the scientific method, it must at least provide adequate data for making reasonable decisions regarding further changes.

Termination of the OD Effort

The seven phases of OD practice just described constitute what I consider the primary, sequential actions a practitioner takes in an organization development effort. My list differs slightly in emphasis and labels from the earlier list of Kolb and Frohman (1970), but the phases are essentially the same, with one exception: Kolb and Frohman's "termination" phase. They argue that "the consultant-client relationship is by definition temporary" (Kolb and Frohman, 1970: p. 61), that the effort either succeeds or fails. It it fails, termination is abrupt; if it is successful and the goals are reached, the consultant may not leave so abruptly, but the relationship terminates because there is no further need for consultative help. It should be noted that Kolb and Frohman's seventh step is consistent with the phases of planned change delineated earlier by Lippitt, Watson, and Westley (1958).

I do not include termination in my list of phases for three reasons. First, termination is not an applicable phase for internal OD practitioners. Although they may conclude specific programs and projects with their clients, they should not terminate the relationship. A primary role of internal practitioners is to serve as guardians of the new culture. They help to regulate the social change that has become a new routine in organizational life (Hornstein et al., 1971). This regulation may take a variety of forms, ranging from periodic checks with client managers regarding the continuing effectiveness of changes to more systematic follow-up activities, such as conducting annual surveys, attending a manager's staff meetings as a process consultant, or helping to design and conduct off-site planning or diagnostic meetings for departments or divisions.

The second reason concerns external OD consultants. A termination phase is and should be more common for external consultants than for internal ones, but it is not necessarily a requirement for effective consultation. A major goal of an external OD consultant is to see that internal resources are established for the kind of help he or she is providing. As soon as possible, internal practitioners should begin to take over the work the external consultant initiates. Thus, although the external consultant's activities with the client organization may decrease, they do not necessarily have to be terminated. Kolb and Frohman's argument for termination is to prevent the client from becoming dependent on the consultant. As an external consultant I have had long-standing relationships with some clients, but I have never experienced these relationships as a great dependency on me. Although dependency may occur as a problem in personal therapy, it rarely becomes an issue in consultation with organizations. I know of consultant-client relationships that have continued for more than a decade, and I consider them healthy and useful for both parties. An organization has a constant need for periodic, objective diagnostic check-ups by external consultants — a need that exists, incidentally, whether or not the organization's managers see it.

Finally, I do not think a termination phase is appropriate because, when OD practitioners follow the action research model, they naturally generate new data for further diagnosis and action. The process is cyclical (French, 1969), and since an organization is both dynamic and naturally follows the entropic process, there is always a great deal of consultative work to be done.

Phases, Not Steps

Phases is a more appropriate term than steps for describing the flow of events in OD work. *Steps* implies discrete actions, while phases better connotes the reality of OD practice: a cycle of changes. Although it is useful for our understanding of OD practice to conceive of distinct phases, in actual practice they blend, overlap, and do not always follow one from the other. Diagnosis, for example, comes early in the OD process and intervention later, but when one is collecting information from the organization for diagnostic purposes, an intervention is occurring simultaneously; when the OD practitioner begins to ask questions about the organization and its members, he or she is intervening.

Phases is an appropriate term also because of the cyclical nature of the OD process. As the process continues, new or undisclosed data are discovered. These data affect organization members, and the members react, creating additional information for diagnosis. Further action is then planned as a consequence of the new, perhaps more refined diagnosis.

Another implication of the cyclical nature of OD relates to the characteristics of open social systems, as delineated by Katz and Kahn (1978). Two of these characteristics are relevant, the notion that organizations proceed through cycles of events over time and the notion that systems seek equilibrium. The first characteristic, that organizational life runs in cycles, is precisely the reason that OD is cyclical. Since organizations are cyclical, OD must also be in order to respond in an appropriate and timely manner. Major events in organizations — planning, budgeting, quarterly reports — are repeated over time; as these events are repeated, new data are likely to be generated each time. Two quarterly reports are rarely the same, and plans and budgets change continuously. Consequently, the diagnosis of an organization in December will be at least somewhat different from the diagnosis conducted the previous June, significantly different if a significant intervention has occurred during the six-month interim. If things in the organization are significantly different six months later, and if these differences are disturbing to organization members, they will seek equilibrium, a return to the former state. Organization development involves change. When change occurs in one of the organization's components or subsystems, other subsystems act to restore the balance. Pressure is brought to bear on organizational behavior that is different from the norm, the organization's culture as it has evolved. Thus, in OD practice, for change to last, recurring diagnoses must be undertaken to determine the state of earlier interventions, and further actions (interventions) are usually needed to reinforce the new behaviors. The long-run objective is to institutionalize the change so that possibilities of changing the OD change will be resisted within the normal pattern of open-system life, which is a pattern of equilibrium seeking.

Summary

In this chapter we have considered the three background models for any OD effort and the seven primary phases of organization development consultation using a case example to illustrate the phases. Although it is instructive to consider these phases — entry, contracting, diagnosis, feedback, planning change, intervention, and evaluation — as discrete steps, and although the consultative flow of events essentially follows the order of the seven phases, in practice the phases are not discrete; they blend together and overlap. When the consultant enters the client organization to collect information by interviews, questionnaires, or observation, the intervention phase, sixth among the ordered group of seven, has already begun. And although evaluation is listed as last, it begins at the entry stage as far as the client is concerned.

These phases are therefore guides for OD consultation. They are highly useful for planning and for ordering sequences of activities and events, but they should not be considered as discrete, rigid steps to follow or as the only phases of consultation in organization development.

Finally, it should be remembered that these guides help to accomplish primary objectives of any OD effort. That is, as OD practitioners we are concerned with *providing people with choices*, so that their feelings of freedom will not be unduly curtailed and thus their resistance will be minimized, and *involving people* at some level of participative decision making and communication regarding the direction of organizational change, so that *commitment* to change implementation will be enhanced.

5

Understanding Organizations
The Process of Diagnosis

Without a framework for understanding the information an OD practitioner collects about a client organization, the data may be nothing more than a mass of confusion — merely an array of comments from a variety of people, representing nothing more than who said what about whom and never rising above the individual and personal level. For information about the organization to become understandable and workable, it must be treated in organizational terms. As noted earlier, organization development represents a systematic approach to change, and the data for diagnosis are largely in systems language; the categories for diagnosis are systems labels.

In this chapter we shall cover selected models of and theories about organizations. These models and theories are useful in the diagnostic phase of OD consultation because they help to organize and systematize the potential mass of confusion. The OD practitioner may choose from a number of models and theories, some that are merely descriptive and others that emphasize dimensions for diagnosis, therefore providing direction for change. The purpose of this chapter is not only to explain some of these models and theories but also to provide the practitioner with some criteria and bases for making choices.

I have been selective in my choice of models and theories to be considered in this chapter. First, I have chosen only those that are behavior-oriented. There are a number of other frameworks or models of organizations, some emphasizing technological aspects, others financial aspects, and still others in informational terms. Organization development practitioners must rely on behavior-oriented models, however, because the role of the OD practitioner is to understand what *people* do or do not do in organizations, not what machines do. The man–machine interface is of definite interest, but only in terms of its consequences for the people involved. Word processing in the office of the future, for example, is of interest to OD practitioners, but only in terms of the changes people will have to make, not for the electronic wizardry involved (Lodahl and Williams, 1978).

We shall explore a number of models for OD purposes. Although they differ from one another, all are based on the open-system notion of input-throughput-output, and all recognize that an organization exists in an environmental context and is a sociotechnical system. Some models place more emphasis on environmental factors than do others, and some stress certain dimensions of organizations, such as structure, more than others do, but they all recognize the same fundamentals — an open system that exists in an environment and consists of people and technology.

We shall first examine three models that are largely descriptive: a model of simplicity with structure, a model of complexity with structure, and a develop-your-own model.

Weisbord's Six-Box Model

A model is useful when it helps us *visualize* reality, and Weisbord's (1976, 1978) model meets this criterion very well. Weisbord depicts his model as a radar screen, with "blips" that tell us about organizational highlights and issues good and bad; but, as air traffic controllers use radar, we too must focus primarily on the screen as a whole, not on individual blips (see Fig. 5–1).

Every organization is situated within an environment and,

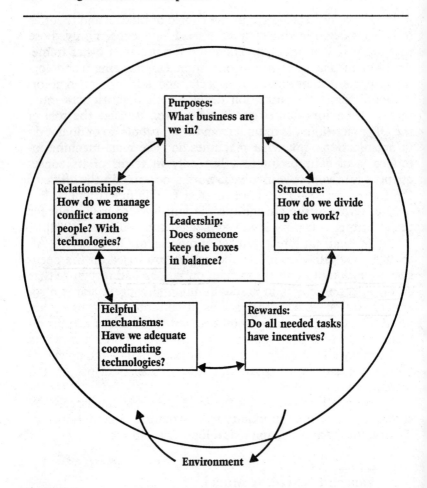

Figure 5–1
Weisbord's Six-Box Organizational Model

Source: M. R. Weisbord, "Organizational Diagnosis: Six Places to Look for Trouble with or without a Theory," *Group and Organization Studies* 1(1976): 430–447. Reprinted by permission.

as the arrows in the figure indicate, is influenced by and in turn has an impact on various elements of that environment. In Weisbord's model, the organization is represented by six boxes: purpose, structure, rewards, helpful mechanisms, relationships, and leadership. Weisbord believes that, for each box, the client organization should be diagnosed in terms of both its formal and its informal systems. A key aspect of any organizational diagnosis is the gap between the formal dimensions of an organization, such as the organization chart (the structure box), and its informal policies, such as how authority is actually exercised. The larger this gap, the more likely it is that the organization is functioning ineffectively.

Weisbord provides key diagnostic questions for each of the six boxes. For the *purposes* box, the two most important factors are goal clarity, the extent to which organization members are clear about the organization's mission and purpose, and goal agreements, whether people support the organization's purpose. For *structure*, the primary question is whether there is an adequate fit between the purpose and the internal structure that is supposed to serve that purpose. With respect to *relationships*, Weisbord contends that three types are most important: between individuals, between units or departments that perform different tasks, and between the people and the nature and requirements of their jobs. He also states that the OD consultant should "diagnose first for required interdependence, then for *quality of relations*, and finally for modes of conflict management" (Weisbord, 1976: p. 440).

In determining possible blips for the *rewards* box, the consultant should diagnose the similarities and differences between what the organization formally rewards (the compensation package, incentive systems, and the like) and what organization members *feel* they are rewarded or punished for doing.

Weisbord places the *leadership* box in the middle because he believes that a primary job of the leader is to watch for blips among the other boxes and to maintain balance among them. To help the OD consultant in diagnosing the leadership box, Weisbord refers to an important book published some years ago by Selznick (1957), citing the four most important leadership tasks. According to Selznick, the consultant should determine the extent to which organizations' leaders are 1) defining purposes,

2) embodying purposes in programs, 3) defending the organization's integrity, and 4) maintaining order with respect to internal conflict.

For the last box, *helpful mechanisms*, Weisbord refers analogously to "the cement that binds an organization together to make it more than a collection of individuals with separate needs" (Weisbord, 1976: p. 443). Thus, helpful mechanisms are the processes that every organization must attend to in order to survive: planning, control, budgeting, and other information systems that help organization members accomplish their respective jobs and meet organizational objectives. The OD consultant's task is to determine which mechanisms (or which aspects of them) help members accomplish organizational purposes and which seem to hinder more than they help. When a helpful mechanism becomes red tape, it probably is no longer helpful.

Table 5–1 gives a summary of the six-box model and the diagnostic questions to be asked.

In summary, Weisbord's model is particularly useful 1) when the consultant does not have as much time as would be desirable for diagnosis, 2) when a relatively uncomplicated organizational map is needed for quick service, or 3) when the client is unaccustomed to thinking in systems terms. In the latter case, the model helps the client to visualize his or her organization as a systemic whole without the use of strange terminology. I have also found Weisbord's model particularly useful in supervising and guiding students in their initial OD consultations.

The Nadler–Tushman Congruence Model

For a more sophisticated client and when more time is available, a more complex model of organizations might be useful for OD diagnosis. In such instances, the Nadler and Tushman (1977) congruence model should serve the purpose.

Nadler and Tushman make the same assumptions as Weisbord — that an organization is an open system and therefore is influenced by its environment (inputs) and also shapes its environment to some extent by outputs. An organization thus is the

Table 5-1

Weisbord's Matrix for Survey Design or Data Analysis

	Formal System (Work To Be Done)	Informal System (Process of Working)
1. Purposes	Goal clarity	Goal agreement
2. Structure	Functional, program, or matrix?	How is work actually done or not done?
3. Relationships	Who should deal with whom on what? Which technologies should be used?	How well do they do it? Quality of relations? Modes of conflict management?
4. Rewards (incentives)	Explicit system What is it?	Implicit, psychic rewards What do people *feel* about payoffs?
5. Leadership	What do top people manage?	How? Normative "style" of administration?
6. Helpful mechanisms	Budget system Management information (measures?) Planning Control	What are they actually used for? How do they function in practice? How are systems subverted?

Diagnostic questions may be asked on two levels:
1. How big a gap is there between formal and informal systems? (This speaks to the fit between individual and organization.)
2. How much discrepancy is there between "what is" and "what ought to be"? (This highlights the fit between organization and environment.)

Source: M. R. Weisbord, "Organizational Diagnosis: Six Places to Look for Trouble with or without a Theory," *Group and Organization Studies* 1(1976): 430–447. Reprinted by permission.

transformation entity between inputs and outputs. Figure 5–2 represents the Nadler–Tushman congruence model.

Inputs

Nadler and Tushman view inputs to the system as relatively fixed; the four they cite are the *environment,* the *resources*

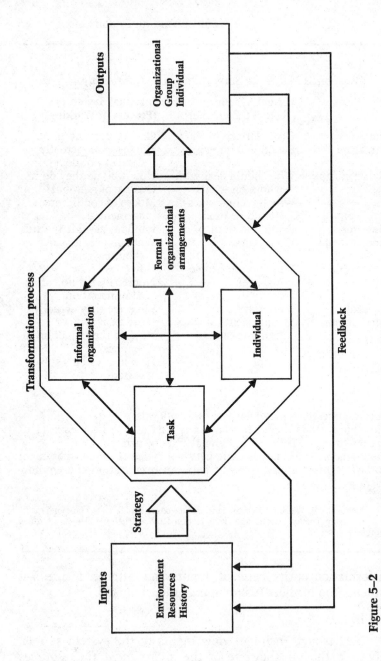

Figure 5–2
The Nadler–Tushman Congruence Model for Diagnosing Organizational Behavior *

available to the organization, the organization's *history*, and *strategies* that are developed and evolve over time. These inputs help define how people in the organization behave, and they serve as constraints on behavior as well as opportunities for action.

As we know from the works of Burns and Stalker (1961), and Lawrence and Lorsch (1967), the extent to which an organization's environment is relatively stable or dynamic significantly affects internal operations, structure, and policy. For many organizations a very important aspect of environment is the parent system and its directives. Such organizations are subsidiaries or divisional profit centers of larger corporations, colleges within a university, or hospitals within a larger health care delivery system. These subordinate organizations may operate relatively autonomously with respect to the outside world (having their own purchasing operations, for example) but because of corporate policy may be fairly restricted in how much money they can spend. Thus, for many organizations we must think of their environments in at least two categories: the larger parent system and the rest of the outside world, including government regulations, competitors, and the marketplace in general.

Resources within the Nadler–Tushman model are capital (money, property, equipment, and so on), raw materials, technologies, people, and various intangibles, such as company name, which may have a high value in the company's market.

An organization's history is also input to the system. The history determines, for example, patterns of employee behavior, policy, the types of people the organization attracts and recruits, and even how decisions get made in a crisis.

Although strategy is categorized as an input in the models, Nadler and Tushman set it apart. Strategy is the process of determining how the organization's resources are best used within the environment for optimal organizational functioning. It is the

---

Source: D. A. Nadler and M. L. Tushman, "A Diagnostic Model for Organization Behavior," in *Perspectives on Behavior in Organizations,* edited by J. R. Hackman, E. E. Lawler, and L. W. Porter (New York: McGraw-Hill, 1977), p. 92. Reprinted by permission.

act of identifying opportunities in the environment and determining whether the organization's resources are adequate for capitalizing on these opportunities. History plays a subtle but influential role in this strategic process.

Some organizations emphasize strategy; that is, they plan. Other organizations simply react to changes in their environments or act opportunistically rather than according to a long-range plan that determines which opportunities will be seized and which will be allowed to pass. As Nadler and Tushman point out, however, organizations have strategies whether they are deliberate and formal or unintentional and informal.

Outputs

We shall move to the right-hand side of the model to consider outputs before covering the transformation process. Thus we shall examine the organization's environment from the standpoint of how it influences the system and how the organization operates internally.

For diagnostic purposes, Nadler and Tushman present four key categories of outputs: system functioning, group behavior, intergroup relations, and individual behavior and effect. With respect to the effectiveness of the system's functioning as a whole, the following three questions should elicit the necessary information:

1. How well is the organization attaining its desired goals of production, service, return on investment, and so on?
2. How well is the organization utilizing its resources?
3. How well is the organization coping with changes in its environment over time?

The remaining three outputs are more directly behavioral: how well groups or units within the organization are performing; how effectively these units communicate with one another, resolve differences, and collaborate when necessary; and how individuals behave. For this last output, individual behavior, we are interested in such matters as turnover, absenteeism, and of course, individual job performance.

The Transformation Process

The components of the transformation process and their interactions are what we normally think of when we consider an organization — the people, the various tasks and jobs, the organization's managerial structure (the organization chart), and all the relationships of individuals, groups, and subsystems. As Fig. 5–2 shows, four interactive major components compose the transformation process that changes inputs into outputs.

The *task component* consists of the jobs to be done and the inherent characteristics of the work itself. The primary task dimensions are the extent and nature of the required interdependence between and among task performers, the level of skill needed, and the kinds of information required to perform the tasks adequately.

The *individual component* consists of all the differences and similarities among employees, particularly demographic data, skill and professional levels, and personality-attitudinal variables.

Organizational arrangements include the managerial and operational structure of the organization, work flow and design, the reward system, management information systems, and the like. These arrangements are the formal mechanisms used by management to direct and control behavior and to organize and accomplish the work to be done.

The fourth component, *informal organization*, is the social structure within the organization, including the grapevine, the organization's internal politics, and the informal authority-information structure (whom you see for what).

Congruence: The Concept of Fit

As Nadler and Tushman point out, a mere listing and description of these system inputs, outputs, and components is insufficient for modeling an organization. An organization is dynamic, never static, and the model must represent this reality, as the arrows in Fig. 5–2 do. Nadler and Tushman go beyond depicting relationships, however. Their term, *fit*, is a measure of the congruence between pairs of inputs and especially between the components of the transformation process. They contend that inconsistent fits between any pair will result in less than optimal organizational and individual performance. Nadler and Tushman's hypothesis, therefore, is that the better the fit, the more effective the organization will be.

Nadler and Tushman recommend three steps for diagnosis:

1. *Identify the system.* Is the system for diagnosis an autonomous organization, a subsidiary, a division, or a unit of some larger system? What are the boundaries of the system, its membership, its tasks, and — if it is part of a larger organization — its relationships with other units?
2. *Determine the nature of the key variables.* What are the dimensions of the inputs and components? What are the desired outputs?
3. *Diagnose the state of fits.* This is the most important step, involving two related activities: a) determining fits between components and b) diagnosing the link between the fits and the organization's outputs.

The OD consultant must concentrate on the degree to which the key components are congruent with one another. Questions such as the following should be asked:

- To what extent do the organizational arrangements fit with the requirements of the task?
- To what extent do individual skills and needs fit with task requirements, with organizational arrangements, and with the informal organization? Hackman and Oldham's (1975) job characteristics theory is a useful supplementary model for this part of the diagnosis, as is expectancy theory (Vroom, 1964; Lawler, 1973).
- To what extent do task requirements fit with both the formal and the informal organization? Information-processing models are useful supplements for this aspect of the diagnosis (Galbraith, 1977; Tushman and Nadler, 1978).

In diagnosing the link between fits and outputs, the OD consultant must focus the outcome of the diagnoses of the various component fits and their behavioral consequences on the set of behaviors associated with systems outputs: goal attainment, resource utilization, and overall systems performance. Considering the component fits, or lack thereof, in light of system outputs helps identify critical problems of the organization. As these problems are addressed and changes are made, the system is then monitored through the feedback loop for purposes of evaluation.

Hornstein and Tichy's Emergent Pragmatic Model

The emergent pragmatic model of organizational diagnosis (Hornstein and Tichy, 1973; Tichy, Hornstein, and Nisberg, 1977) is based on the premise that most managers and consultants "carry around in their heads" implicit theories or models about organizational behavior and about how human systems actually operate. These notions are usually intuitive, ill-formed, and difficult to articulate. Because they are largely intuitive, different observers and members of organizations have different theories, which gives rise to conflicts among consultants or between consultants and clients about what is really wrong with the organization and how to fix it.

To deal with these intuitive notions, Hornstein and Tichy have developed a procedure for helping managers and consultants articulate and eventually conceptualize their implicit models and therefore make them explicit. The procedure, known as an emergent pragmatic theory or model, consists of using a workbook and selecting items from among twenty-two sample labels or creating one's own labels from twenty-eight blank labels that are provided. These labels include such items as informal groupings, fiscal characteristics, turnover, goals, and satisfaction of members with their jobs. Individuals' selections represent the information they would seek in diagnosing an organization.

Hornstein and Tichy's approach to organizational diagnosis is one that is shared between consultant and client and among members of the client organization. The approach is identified as an emergent pragmatic theory because "the model *emerges* from an exploration of both the consultant's and client's assumptions about behavior and organizations . . . and draws on both the consultant's and client's organizational *experiences* as well as on empirical and theoretical work in the field" (Tichy, Hornstein, and Nisberg, 1977: p. 367, emphasis added).

Another of Hornstein and Tichy's premises is that, consciously or not, organizational consultants tend to impose their theories and models of human systems on their clients. These impositions may or may not fit with the client members' perceptions and beliefs, and may or may not jibe with the client organization's underlying values. To assure better congruence, Hornstein and Tichy advocate a highly collaborative approach between consultants and clients, one that results in an emergent model that represents different perspectives and experiences.

There are five phases to the emergent-pragmatic approach. The consultant guides the client group through these phases:

1. Exploring and Developing a Diagnostic Model. The first step of this phase is for members of the client group to work individually in the workbooks and select labels from the workbook for the organizational items that represent the most important dimensions of organization for the purpose of diagnosis, at least from each individual's point of view.

The second step of this initial phase is for all members of the client group to agree on a common list. This agreement process consists largely of eliminating overlapping labels and arriving at a final list that represents all individuals' selections.

The third step is to develop categories of organizational components from the common list of labels. This step is a group activity. Categories of labels representing organizational components might include such elements as formal structure, hard data (for example, a profit-and-loss statement), environmental interface, and organization member characteristics. A secondary but important consequence of this step is that the group begins to develop a common language, a shared organizational vocabulary. The terms and categories are therefore concrete, pragmatic, and more meaningful for the client members.

The final step of this initial phase is to make the model dynamic. For this activity, the group members first imagine that change may occur in one component of their model and then trace the effects of this change on all other components. They do this for each component of their model. The resulting matrix shows which components the group members believe are the most and the least significant in terms of impact on other components. The model is then used as the basis for developing change strategies.

2. Developing Change Strategies. Since different components of the model will probably have different impacts, client members are in a position to determine potential levers for change. "For instance, if a model included a category called formal structure which contained such items as authority structure, reward system, and formal communication structure, the category produced desirable changes in a number of other categories" (Tichy, Hornstein, and Nisberg, 1977: p. 372). Thus, the strategy is a statement of a plan for what is to be changed, the method of change, and the sequence of events comprising the change steps.

3. Developing Change Techniques. This phase consists of exploring potential techniques, determining which are most appropriate, and then matching the selected techniques with each organizational component that has been designated for change.

4. Assessing the Necessary Conditions for Assuring Success. The final selection of change techniques is based on criteria developed in this phase. These criteria usually stem from such conditions as the system's readiness for change, the available resources, budget considerations, and the system's history regarding change, especially whether OD has been attempted before.

5. Evaluating the Change Strategies. For this final phase, criteria are developed for evaluating the success or failure of the overall change strategy, and measurement procedures are developed.

The emergent pragmatic approach to organizational diagnosis is based on two assumptions: 1) that most managers and consultants have intuitive theories about how organizations function, rather than well-formed conceptual frameworks; and 2) that many consultants impose their models and theories on client organizations, regardless of how appropriate they may be for the particular client. Hornstein and Tichy advocate a collaborative model of diagnosis to avoid the potential negative consequences of operating on the basis of these two assumptions.

The two models described earlier, Weisbord's six-box model and the Nadler–Tushman congruence model, are generic frameworks and do not fall prey to the problems of Hornstein and Tichy's two premises. When the consultant and the client do not find the Weisbord, Nadler–Tushman, or other formal models to their liking, however, the emergent pragmatic approach offers a clear alternative. It is a do-it-yourself model, and, if both consultant and client are willing to spend the time required to do it right, a mutually satisfying and appropriate model for the client organization is likely to result.

The three models described may all be categorized as *contingency* models; they do not specify directions for change prior to diagnosis. What needs to be changed emanates from the diagnosis. None of the models advocates a particular design for an organization's internal structure, a certain style of behavior, or a specific approach to management. The inventors of these models do have biases, however. Weisbord says the boxes should be in balance, Nadler and Tushman argue that the various dimensions of their model should fit with one another, and Hornstein and Tichy state that the consultant and client should collaborate toward the emergence of a model that is appropriate for the given organization. These biases have more to do with the best way to diagnose than with the most important dimension to change.

Lawrence and Lorsch's Contingency Theory

Lawrence and Lorsch, early contingency advocates, specify neither a best way to diagnose nor a particular direction for change. They do emphasize certain dimensions of organization however, particularly structure and intergroup relationships. They consider other dimensions, but these two take priority in their view of organizations.

Lawrence and Lorsch do not have a model of organizations as such, and thus they may be classified more appropriately as contingency theorists. They argue (or hypothesize) that there is a cause-and-effect relationship between how well an organization's internal structure matches environmental demands and how well the organization performs — that is, accomplishes goals and objectives. Their research in the 1960s provided support for their argument (Lawrence and Lorsch, 1967).

For the present purposes, we want to understand the use of their contingency theory for diagnosis. Keep in mind that the primary concepts of the Lawrence and Lorsch contingency theory are differentiation and integration. These two concepts represent the paradox of any organization design, that labor must simultaneously be divided and coordinated or integrated. Within the Lawrence and Lorsch framework and for diagnostic purposes, therefore, we want to examine a client organization along the dimensions the client considers to be important. The methodological appendix of their book provides considerable detail concerning these dimensions and the questions to ask for obtaining the relevent information (Lawrence and Lorsch, 1967). The following list summarizes these dimensions and some of the related questions.

Environmental Demands

1. On what basis does a customer evaluate and choose between competing suppliers in this industry (price, quality, delivery, service, and so forth)?
2. What are the major problems an organization encounters when competing in this industry?
3. Have there been significant changes in the market or technical conditions in this industry in recent years?

Differentiation

1. Regarding structure, what is the average span of control? How important is it to have formal rules for routing procedures and operations?
2. Regarding the time span of feedback, how long does it take for employees to see the results of their performance? (In sales, for example, the time lag is typically short, whereas in research and development it may take years.)

3. Regarding interpersonal relationships, how important are they, and how much interaction is necessary?
4. Regarding goal certainty, how clear-cut are the goals? How are they measured?

Integration

1. How interdependent are any two units: high (each depends on the other for survival); medium (each needs some things from the other); or low (each functions fairly autonomously)?
2. What is the quality of relations between units?

Conflict Management

1. What mode of conflict resolution is used: forcing (top-down edicts); smoothing (being kind and avoiding); or confronting (exposing differences and solving problems)?
2. How much influence do employees have on the hierarchy for solving problems and making decisions?

Employee–Management Contract

1. To what extent do employees feel that what is expected of them is appropriate?
2. To what extent do employees feel that they are compensated and rewarded fairly for their performance?

Summary

These five dimensions represent the organizational domains that Lawrence and Lorsch believe most important for effective diagnosis. Based on their research findings, the organizational diagnostician would be looking for the degree of match between environmental demands and complexities and the internal organizational structure. The greater the environmental complexity, the more complex the internal design should be. If the organization's markets change rapidly and are difficult to predict and forecast, and if the environment in general fluctuates considerably, the organization's internal structure should be relatively decentralized so that many employees can be in touch with the environment and can act quickly as changes occur. Under these conditions, differentiation may still be high, but a premium is placed on integration. There must be sufficient integrating mechanisms so that communication flows adequately across and among the many subunits and so that superiors in the hierarchy are kept well informed. The plastics industry represented this type of organization in the Lawrence and Lorsch research study. When the environment is relatively stable and not particularly complex, as in the container industry in their study, a fairly simple and straightforward internal structure may be best, with functional division of labor and centralized authority.

The issue is not whether one organization should be highly differentiated and another highly integrated but that they should be highly differentiated *and* integrated. High integration seems to be important regardless of environment, and differentiation may be lower for organizations with stable environments. The paradox remains in any case: both are needed, but they are antagonistic — the more the organization is differentiated, the more integration is required.

The organizational diagnostician should also seek the mode of conflict resolution. Lawrence and Lorsch found that the more organization members and units confront their differences and work to resolve them, rather than smoothing them over or squashing them with edicts from on high, the more effective the organization tended to be.

Finally, it is necessary to know the degree of employees' satisfaction with their psychological contract with the organization. There is apparently a positive relationship between clarity of employees' understanding of what is expected of them — their perceived satisfaction with the rewards they receive for performance — and overall organizational performance.

Although Lawrence and Lorsch are contingency theorists, particularly with respect to organization structure, they too have their biases. They stress interfaces — between the organization and its environment, between and among units within the organization, and between individual employees and the organization as represented by management.

Normative Theories

Unlike contingency theorists, normative theorists argue that, for organization development, there is one best way to and direction for change. Major proponents of normative theory are Likert (1967) and Blake and Mouton (1968a, 1978).

Likert's Profiles

Likert categorizes organizations, or systems in his terms, as one of four types:

> System 1. Autocratic, top-down, exploitative management
>
> System 2. Benevolent autocracy, still top-down but not as exploitive
>
> System 3. Consultative (Employees are consulted about problems and decisions but management still makes the final decisions.)
>
> System 4. Participative management (Key policy decisions are made in groups by consensus.)

Likert's approach to organizational diagnosis is standardized. The mode used is a questionnaire, the "Profile of Organizational Characteristics," with six sections: leadership, motivation, communication, decisions, goals, and control. (The latest version is labeled the "Survey of Organizations.") Organization members answer questions in each of these sections by placing the letter N at the place on a twenty-point scale that best represents their opinion now and a P at the place that indicates their previous opinion — how they experienced their organization one or two years ago. Sometimes the consultant asks organization members to use an I instead of a P, to indicate what they would consider ideal for each of the questions.

Organizational profiles typically range in the System 2 or System 3 categories. If the ideal response is used, its profile will usually occur to the right of the now profile, toward or within

System 4. In such cases, the direction for change is established, toward System 4.

When one declares that there is one best way, in this case System 4 management, others usually demand evidence. Is System 4 management a better way to run an organization than System 3 or 2 or 1? Contingency theorists, of course, would say no; it depends on the type of business the organization is in, the nature of the environment the organization faces, and the technology involved. Likert contends that, regardless of these contingencies, System 4 is best. Likert's (1967) own research supports his claim, and so does research by others. A longitudinal study of perhaps the most systematic change to System 4 management — conducted in the Harwood-Weldon Company, a manufacturer of sleepwear — is a noteworthy example (Marrow, Bowers, and Seashore, 1967). Changes were made in all dimensions of Likert's profile as well as in work flow and organizational structure. The durability of these changes was supported by a later study conducted by Seashore and Bowers (1970).

A System 4 approach was also used as the change goal for a General Motors assembly plant (Dowling, 1975). As a result of these deliberate change efforts toward System 4, significant improvements were accomplished on several indexes, including operating efficiency, costs, and grievances.

In summary, Likert's approach to organizational diagnosis is structured and directional. It is structured by use of his questionnaire, the "Profile of Organizational Characteristics," and of later versions of his profile (Taylor and Bowers, 1972), and it is directional in that data that are collected are compared with System 4. The survey feedback method (to be explained in the next chapter) is used as the main intervention; that is, the data from the questionnaire (survey) are reported back to organizational members in a set manner.

In order to use Likert's approach, the consultant should feel comfortable with the questionnaire method as the primary mode for data gathering and with System 4 management as the goal for change. Although participative management may feel comfortable as a change goal for many consultants and clients, the relatively limited diagnosis by profile characteristics only may not be so comfortable.

Blake and Mouton's Grid® Method of Organization Development

The other normative approach to OD is based on the Managerial Grid Model developed by Blake and Mouton (1964, 1978). Like Likert's System 4 approach, the Grid method of OD is structured and involves a high degree of packaging. Blake and Mouton also argue that there is one best way to manage an organization. Their label is 9,9, which also represents a participative style of management.

Blake and Mouton also depend on questionnaires, but Grid OD (Blake and Mouton, 1968a) goes far beyond an initial diagnosis with a questionnaire. Blake and Mouton start from an initial, general diagnosis. In a cross-cultural study of what managers consider the most common barriers to business effectiveness and corporate excellence, Blake and Mouton (1968a) found that communication topped the list of ten, and a lack of planning was second. These two barriers were selected by managers much more frequently than the remaining eight (74% noted communication and 62% mentioned planning); morale and coordination, for example, the next most frequently mentioned barriers, were noted by less than 50%. Blake and Mouton further pointed out that communication and planning were the top two mentioned regardless of country, company, or characteristics of the managers reporting. These two major barriers, and the other less prevalent ones, are symptoms of organizational problems, not causes, according to Blake and Mouton. The causes lie deeper in the system. Faulty planning, for example, is a result of an organization's not having a strategy or having a strategy that is based on unsound rationale. Communication problems derive from the nature of the supervision practiced in the organization.

For addressing these underlying causes, Blake and Mouton have developed a six-phase approach to organization development that considers both the organization's strategic plan, or lack thereof, and the style or approach to supervision or management. They contend that, to achieve excellence, an organizational strategic model should be developed and the supervisory style should be changed in the direction of participative management. Organization members should first examine managerial behavior and style and then move on to develop and implement an ideal strategic organizational model. Before explaining the six phases of their OD approach in more detail, we should consider Blake and Mouton's managerial style model, the Managerial Grid, because most of their normative rationale is based on this model.

Building on earlier research work on leadership, in which the dual functions of a leader were variously labeled as initiation of structure and consideration, task and maintenance, and task and socioemotional behaviors, Blake and Mouton (1964) simplified the language by using terms closer to managers' understanding: *production* and *people*. They did more, however; the creative aspect of their work was to conceptualize each of the two leader functions on a continuum, one for the manager's degree of concern for production and one for his or her concern for people, and to put the two together in the form of a graph, a two-dimensional model.

Blake and Mouton (1981) contend that they have done more than merely simplifying the language and creating nine-point scales. They argue that the original dimensions — initiation of structure and consideration — and those that followed, especially Hersey and Blanchard's situational leadership model, were conceptualized as independent dimensions. Blake and Mouton's dimensions — production and people — are interdependent, however, and represent attitudes more than behavior. They note that leadership is not possible without both task and people. We shall now consider Blake and Mouton's model in more detail.

Any manager will have some degree of concern for accomplishing the organization's purpose of producing products or services — that is, a concern for production, results, or profits. A manager will also have some degree of concern for the people who are involved in helping to accomplish the organization's purpose. Managers may differ in how concerned they are with each of these managerial functions, but how these two concerns mesh for a given manager determines his or her *style* or approach to management and defines that manager's use of power.

Blake and Mouton chose nine-point scales to depict their model and to rank the manager's degree of concern for production and people; 1 represents a low concern and 9 indicates a high concern. Although there are eighty-one possible combinations, Blake and Mouton realistically chose to consider only the four more or less extreme positions, represented in the four corners of the grid, and the middle-of-the-road style, position 5,5 in the middle of the grid. Figure 5–3 illustrates the managerial grid.

Blake and Mouton describe the five styles as follows:

9,1. In the lower right-hand corner of the Grid a maximum concern (9) for production is combined with a minimum concern (1) for people. A manager acting under these assumptions concentrates on maximizing production by exercising power and authority and achieving control over people through compliance.

1,9. Here a minimum concern (1) for production is coupled with a maximum concern (9) for people. Primary attention is placed on promoting good feelings among colleagues and subordinates.

1,1. A minimum concern for both production and people is represented by 1,1 in the lower left corner. [This] manager does only the minimum required to remain within the organization.

5,5. This is the "middle-of-the-road" theory or the "go-along-to-get-along" assumptions which are revealed in conformity to status quo.

9,9. Production and people concerns are integrated at a high level. . . . This is the team approach. It is goal-oriented and seeks to gain results of high quantity and quality through participation, involvement, commitment, and conflict-solving. (Blake and Mouton, 1978: p. 12)

As noted earlier, Blake and Mouton contend that communication problems in the organization stem from the nature of supervision. The predominant style of supervisors in American organizations today can be characterized as 5,5 (Blake and Mouton, 1978). The popular book *The Gamesman* (Maccoby, 1976) is a description of Blake and Mouton's 5,5 manager. An unpublished study by a colleague, Barry Render, and I also found 5,5 to be the predominant style of middle managers in a large government agency ($N = 400$). This style, according to Blake and Mou-

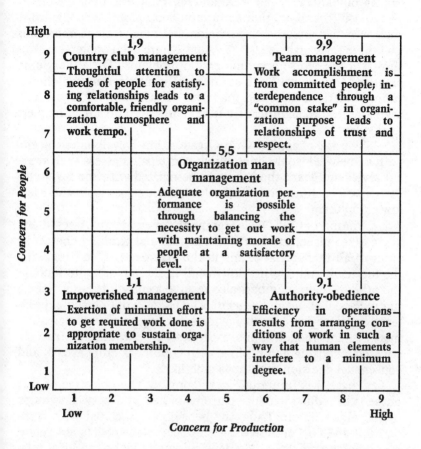

Figure 5–3
The Managerial Grid®

Source: The Managerial Grid figure from *The Managerial Grid III: The Key to Leadership Excellence*, by Robert R. Blake and Jane Srygley Mouton. Houston: Gulf Publishing Company, Copyright © 1985, page 12. Reproduced by permission.

ton, is bureaucratic and mechanistic, thus less than effective. They posit, therefore, that communication problems come from such less-than-effective supervision and management approach. The three styles labeled 9,1, 1,9, and 1,1 are even poorer, causing similar if not worse communication problems. The 9,9 style, if practiced consistently, will assure significantly fewer problems of communication. Training managers to adopt a 9,9 style will therefore lead to significantly fewer barriers to organizational effectiveness.

The six phases of Grid Organization Development begin with a one-week seminar at which participants assess their present styles and learn the behaviors associated with the 9,9 style. Participants also receive feedback on their styles from their fellow group members.

Phase 2 of Grid OD is teamwork development. Assessment again takes place, to identify the norms and working characteristics of all managerial teams in the organization, starting with the top team and moving downward in the hierarchy to include the others. Team members also receive feedback regarding their interpersonal styles in the team. The teams work on actual problems and practice team behavior according to the participative management model. Thus, openness is encouraged, trust is stressed, exposing and dealing with conflict is emphasized, and consensual decision making is practiced.

Phase 3 is intergroup development. The objective of this phase is to reduce win-lose patterns of behavior between groups in the organization. Thus, the behaviors associated with competition and cooperation are examined. Ideal models are generated, each group separately developing a model of an ideal relationship, and these models are exchanged between groups. Finally, action steps are planned for facilitating the groups' move toward what they jointly decide is an ideal relationship.

Phase 4 is development of an ideal strategic corporate model. This phase is essentially what is called corporate strategic planning. It begins with the development of an ideal strategic organization, usually done by the top management team. This team practices what Blake and Mouton call "strict business logic" as they 1) specify minimum and optimum financial objectives, 2) describe business activities to be pursued in the future, 3) define markets for penetration, 4) create an internal structure for synergistic results, 5) delineate policies to guide future decisions, and 6) identify development requirements for sustaining the model.

Phase 5 is implementation of the ideal strategic model. This phase, similar to what Beckhard and Harris (1977) later called transition management, consists of moving toward the ideal model in a carefully managed, evolutionary manner while continuing to run the organization as before. This continuing-to-run process gradually changes, so that the organization begins to operate more and more within the policies and procedures of the ideal model.

Phase 6 is systematic critique. During this final phase, the change effort is evaluated and so-called drag factors are identified. (*Drag factors* are specific barriers that still exist and must now be overcome.)

Phases 1, 2, and 3 are thus designed to deal with communication barriers to organizational effectiveness, and Phases 4, 5, and 6 deal with the planning barriers.

It is interesting that not until Phase 6 do Blake and Mouton begin to deal with an organization diagnostically in terms like those of the other diagnostic models we have considered. Blake and Mouton have evidently decided that all fairly large organizations that are not already involved in organization development have serious communication and planning barriers to effectiveness. These two primary barriers must be reduced first, and Grid OD will do the job. At Phase 6 we will see how effectively the first five phases have progressed and we will know, *in particular* and *in detail*, what barriers must now be tackled.

Blake and Mouton never state it, but they apparently assume that, unless an organization learns how to communicate more effectively (practice 9,9 management) and plan more logically and systematically (build an ideal strategic model and begin to implement it), its management will never be able to deal optimally with the specifics of running a business. Phase 6 in the grid OD sequence gets to the specifics.

Blake and Mouton refer to their six-volume book, *How to Assess the Strengths and Weaknesses of a Business Enterprise* (1972), as the "Phase 6 Instrument." It is based on their diagnostic model, "Corporate Excellence Rubric," and consists of seventy-two windows — elements that are used to diagnose corporate behavior, performance, and results.

Blake and Mouton's (1968b) book has more than 400 pages of various issues and scales. Phase 6 is obviously time-consuming, detailed, structured, and tedious but very thorough. Although it is highly structured, there is some flexibility in that respondents may rewrite issues to suit their own situations better.

Levinson's Clinical-Historical Approach

Levinson's theory of organization behavior is grounded in psychoanalytic theory and views organizations in familial dimensions: "An organization is composed of persons in authority and 'siblings' who relate to these authorities" (Levinson, 1972a: p. 23). Because it is so closely aligned with psychoanalytic theory, it is not surprising that Levinson's approach to organizational diagnosis (Levinson, 1972a) is very detailed, emphasizes history, and generally relies on clinical methods (Levinson, 1972b). Using Levinson's approach, the consultant does a work-up on a client organization, much as a physician would do with a patient, and obtains as complete a history as possible, especially in terms of how the organization fits into its environment. In the search for information, Levinson (1972a) suggests:

> Most newspapers have morgues, or files of clippings, filed by subject. Historical societies often have much information on file. Large organizations will frequently be the subject of articles in trade or professional magazines which may be located through libraries. . . . The sheer availability of various kinds of information is a datum of diagnostic value. (p. 26)

Physicians collect historical information about their patients and then, in addition to taking such measurements as blood tests, observe their patients and thump here and there to determine what the patients "feel like." Levinson also stresses observation, especially initial impressions of the organization. Levinson notes: "Since the consultant is his own most important instrument, he should begin [his tour of the organization by using] his antennae for sensing subtleties" (1972a: p. 18). Levinson argues that the consultant should request a tour of as much of the organization as time and practicalities will permit so that initial impressions can be made and recorded. "The consultant will find it helpful to keep a diary of his experiences in the company, to record events and observations which will not likely be reported in interviews or questionnaires" (Levinson, 1972a: p. 19).

Levinson (1972a) relies on the following six categories of data for diagnosis.

1. Consultant Observations and Feelings. Notes on how the consultant experiences the organization, especially initial impressions, are recorded and become a set of information for later diagnosis.

2. Factual Data. Recorded policies and procedures, historical data on file in the organization, annual reports, job descriptions, personnel statistics, and former consultant or task force reports are perused. Collecting this information is not enough, according to Levinson; how the data may interrelate is important, as is the type of language used. The language will convey attitudes toward people and assumptions about what motivates employees.

3. Outside Information. Information is collected, primarily through interviews, from the organization's suppliers and competitors, cooperating organizations, agents, professional associations, and the like. This information will help the consultant understand the organization's environment in general and the impact it has on the client.

4. Pattern of Organization. The organization chart and the authority-responsibility structure of the organization are the primary indicators of pattern of organization. Levinson stresses a holistic approach rather than a view of the interaction of just one or two subsystems.

5. Settings. According to Levinson, "First overall organizational purposes and then how these purposes are subdivided into specific functions performed by definable groups within definable temporal and physical space. . . . The consultant must learn where and by whom essential functions of the organization are carried out" (1972a: p. 28).

Levinson refers to Bennis (1959) for a further breakdown of functions in these settings into more specific organizational functions:

> Service activities support functions
>
> Problem-solving settings — collecting and analyzing information, such as production planning
>
> Production activities — the primary throughput between input and output, such as manufacturing
>
> Indoctrination settings — formalized training programs
>
> Control activities — goal setting, monitoring, and evaluating progress

Levinson also notes in this context what Rice (1958) has called the time dimension "temporal boundaries within which the setting's central purpose is accomplished . . . such as factory shift work . . . or . . . planning activities in a management group" (Levinson, 1972a: p. 29).

6. Task Patterns. Group-level variables exist in each setting. Levinson cities four such patterns.

> Complementary activities — contributions of each work group member toward some common goal
>
> Parallel activities — group members performing essentially identical tasks
>
> Sequential activities — group members performing some phase of the overall group task
>
> Individualized activities — unique functions performed by each person

These patterns constitute a setting, and the consultant attempts to learn the setting boundaries by analyzing the task patterns.

It is important to note that, although Levinson's theoretical base is psychological and his method of diagnosis is patterned after the clinical model, he does not become absorbed in pieces of the system. His approach is systemic and holistic. Although he is biased toward a Freudian view, he does not lose himself in the analytic but rather looks for systemic issues and considers how the organization influences and is influenced by its environment, how subparts of the organization relate, and how work flows from one setting, activity, and function to another. Thus, being an organizational diagnostician of the Levinson school would require a thorough grounding in psychoanalytic theory, an understanding of the clinical method of diagnosis, and a systems view of organizations that highlights patterns of relationships and work flow.

Summary

In this chapter we have considered the diagnostic phase of organization development consultation in some depth by examining certain models. These models — Weisbord's six-box model, Nadler and Tushman's congruence models, Hornstein and Tichy's emergent pragmatic model, Lawrence and Lorsch's contingency model, the normative models of Likert and Blake and Mouton, and Levinson's clinical-historical approach — are not the only ones available. For organization development purposes, however, they are the most relevant ones and they demonstrate the diversity of the field. There is considerable choice for the OD practitioner-consultant.

I do not often have the time required for using Levinson's approach, although I like his thoroughness and the systemic-flow perspective. When time is short and my client is naive about systems, Weisbord's six-box model works well. Nadler and Tushman's model is appealing for some of the same reasons as Levinson's, but it is easier to work with and easier to communicate to a client. Hornstein and Tichy's approach is very useful for clients who are concerned that a consultant might impose something on them, and it is useful for setting the stage for in-depth diagnosis. Lawrence and Lorsch's contingency model is currently the most popular one among OD practitioners, and with good reason: it emphasizes organizational structure, which was overlooked by OD people in the early days, and shows how the organization's environment has an internal impact. Likert's and

Blake and Mouton's theories are appealing because they clearly show the way, but if their approaches are chosen, they must be followed completely; a partial application will not work. Their high degree of structure and their normative view turn away some OD practitioners. Under certain circumstances, however, I have found both to be useful. Likert's profile is useful for providing an outside, more objective questionnaire assessment of an organization, and Blake and Mouton's grid for providing a framework for examining managerial style in the organization.

An OD practitioner's choice from among these models should be based primarily on two considerations. First, it is important to use a model effectively if one does not understand it. Second, the practitioner should feel comfortable with the model and its approach. If one does not really believe in participative management, using Likert's or Blake and Mouton's approach is not likely to be successful.

6

Planning and Managing Change

It is easy to write, if not to assume, that diagnosis is one activity and intervention (that is, planning and implementing change) is quite another. In practice, however, this is simply not true. As Schein (1969) pointed out, when one enters a human system to conduct a diagnosis, an intervention in fact is being made.

It is helpful to our understanding, nevertheless, to consider the phases of planning and managing change as following diagnosis and feedback. Thus, once a diagnosis has been made and feedback has been provided to the client, it is time to plan the appropriate steps to take so that problems identified in the diagnostic phase are addressed and a more ideal future state for the organization can be determined. Guiding this planning phase should be a set of coherent and interrelated concepts: a theory, model, a conceptual frame of reference.

This chapter first defines intervention and then covers the planning and management of the change phase in more detail. Finally, we shall consider ways to determine if progress is being made in a change effort.

Chris Argyris (1970) has provided a fairly technical and specific definition of intervention:

> To intervene is to enter into an ongoing system of rela-
> tionships, to come between or among persons, groups, or
> objects for the purpose of helping them. There is an im-
> portant implicit assumption in the definition that should
> be made explicit: the system exists independently of the
> intervenor. (p. 15)

According to Argyris, collecting data from an organization is intervening, which supports Schein's contention and our earlier
claim that the phases of OD are not discrete. For this phase of
organization development, however, we shall think in terms of
some specified activity, some event or planned sequence of events
that occurs as a result of diagnosis and feedback. The process of
moving from a functional way of organizing to a project form, for
example, regardless of how long it takes (and it might take
months) could constitute an OD intervention. Another example
of a possible OD intervention would be a singular event and would
take a comparatively short period of time. Either type of activity
could serve as an OD intervention, provided the event 1) responds
to an actual and felt need for change on the part of the client, 2)
involves the client in the planning and implementing of the
change (intervention), and 3) leads to change in the organization's
culture.

Criteria for Effective Intervention

Argyris (1970) has specified similar criteria for what he
considers the primary tasks of an interventionist (OD practitioner). His three criteria are 1) valid and useful information, 2)
free choice, and 3) internal commitment. By *valid and useful information*, he means "that which describes the factors plus their
interrelationships, that create the problem for the client system"
(Argyris, 1970: p. 17). According to Argyris, the information the
OD practitioner has collected from and about the client accurately reflects what people in the organization perceive and feel,
what they consider to be their primary concerns and issues, what
they experience as complexities and perhaps accompanying frus-
trations of living within and being a part of the client system, and

what they would like to see changed. Argyris goes on to specify that, if several independent diagnoses lead to the same intervention, the data the practitioner has gathered are valid.

For all practical purposes this first task of an interventionist, obtaining valid and useful information, is similar to my first criterion for intervention, responding to an actual and felt need for change on the part of the client. If valid information is obtained by the practitioner, it will reflect a need. If the practitioner responds to that need, he or she will have done so by providing valid and useful information.

By *free choice*, Argyris means that "the locus of decision making [is] in the client system" (1970: p. 19) and that the client is provided alternatives for action. No particular or specified action is automatic, preordained, or imposed. Argyris explains:

> A choice is free to the extent the members can make their selection for a course of action with minimal internal defensiveness; can define the path (or paths) by which the intended consequence is to be achieved; can relate the choice to their central needs; and can build into their choices a realistic and challenging level of aspiration. Free choice therefore implies that the members are able to explore as many alternatives as they consider significant and select those that are central to their needs. (ibid.)

By *internal commitment*, Argyris means that the client owns the choice made and feels responsible for implementing it. Organization members act on their choice because it responds to needs, both individual and on behalf of the organization.

The primary tasks of choice and internal commitment will be accomplished if the practitioner involves the client in planning and implementing the intervention. Argyris does not specify cultural change, my third criterion. He implies that, if the practitioner accomplishes the three primary tasks, the organization's culture will be changed. This is only an implication, however; he does not specify it.

Although there are similarities between Argyris's criteria and mine, the primary difference is that I am expressing processes or means while he is stating end states or outcomes. Either way of expressing these criteria makes sense.

Planning the Intervention or Change

We may or may not agree on the fine points concerning a definition of and the criteria for an effective intervention. Unless there is some readiness for change within the client organization, definitions and criteria are no more than an academic exercise. I have heard Richard Beckhard express it one way and Harry Levinson another, but both essentially said, when it comes to organization (or individual for that matter) change, "no pain, no change." Unless enough key people in the organization feel a real need for change, none is likely to occur, at least none that is planned and managed.

Readiness for Change

Sometimes determining readiness is quite obvious and straightforward. The company's sales have fallen dramatically, costs have risen so sharply that profit doesn't exist anymore, turnover and absenteeism are significantly out of line when compared with others in the same industry, morale has never been lower or the market strategy doesn't seem to work anymore — these are some obvious and rather straightforward examples of a need for change. Under any of these circumstances, it is not difficult to determine a readiness. In other instances, or even in the instances listed above, everyone may not see or understand a need for change. In this situation, the need must be generated. This may be done in either of two ways. One way is to gather information, the facts, about the current situation and contrast this information with where the organization was supposed to have been by this time. In other words, it is a matter of comparing actual achievements with what was desired, the organization's goals or mission.

Assuming that organizational members have identified with these goals (no minor assumption, I should emphasize) and they then see a significant difference between the actual and the desired, they will experience a need to reduce the difference or gap between what is actual and what is desired. In this case, the desired state is known; not known is how far off the mark the organization's actual performance is from that which is desired. Contrasting actual with desired creates the required motivation for change.

Another way to generate awareness of the need for change is to describe a more desirable future state. Organizational members may be satisfied with the status quo and experience no need for change unless and until they are presented with a possibility of something better, more desirable. It might mean a lot of hard work and a considerable modification in the way that work is done, but the new mission and differences in how work would be accomplished may be sufficiently attractive that a motivational pull toward this more desirable future state would be generated.

Even though generating awareness of the need for change may be accomplished in these two different ways, the principle is the same. Presenting people with a discrepancy between what is and what is desired will create tension, and the motivation will be in the direction of reducing that tension, that is, to move toward the more desired state. This principle of human behavior is based on sound theory and research; see, for example, Lewin (1936) or Duvall and Wicklund (1972).

Preparing the client for change, what we have labeled readiness, is what Lewin called the unfreezing stage (see Chapter 4). Unfreezing is creating conditions whereby the client is shaken loose (unfrozen) from the status quo. The client's mental and emotional set has been broken and is therefore more amenable to consider, if not accept, change. For more elaboration on this stage, as well as additions to our understanding of Lewin's next two stages, changing and refreezing, see Schein (1980).

We have also used the terms *actual* and *desired* state. This is the language of Beckhard and Harris (1977). Developing a new mission, a new vision, a fresh image of the future is the process of creating a desired state, a way of being, of working that is more desirable than the present state. Planning any change effort involves this kind of development, i.e., creating an image of the more desired future state. This creative process is not easy to do. Even more difficult, however, is *moving* the organization to that desired future. Beckhard and Harris (1977), based on the earlier thinking of Lewin, view the change process in three "states":

Present State → Transition State → Future State

While determining the future state is obviously critical, Beckhard and Harris concern themselves far more with the transition state, managing the change process, the more difficult phase.

Power and Leadership

In addition to determining readiness and preparing the client organization for change by contrasting actual with desired, other planning activities must occur. It is a leadership function to see to it that the future state is developed. Leaders in the organization need to be far more concerned with determining the future than specifying how to get there. Gaining commitment from organization members to the future state, a plan, is critical; gaining commitment to implementing the plan is even more critical. More will be stated on this latter point in the next section.

A leadership function, therefore, is to make certain that a plan for the future is in place and then to generate energy and enthusiasm within the organization to support the transition.

In any sizable organization formal as well as informal leaders exist. Often overlooked in a change effort is the latter group. It is obvious that senior management needs to be "on board." If unionized, leaders within the union(s) need to be involved and supportive. All of the key managers who head the various boxes on the organization chart need to be on board. Not so obvious, however, are those who informally, from time to time, influence people's opinions. In an organization such as the National Aeronautics and Space Administration, for example, informal leadership comes from scientists and engineers who are not line, operational administrators but who are, as individuals, highly respected. Their opinions about matters are sought and they are influential. If these highly respected, listened-to, powerful individuals are not supportive of the change effort, resistance among organizational members will be greater than would otherwise be the case. It is wise, therefore, early in the planning process, to engage these informal leaders in discussing what change is needed and what is more desirable for the future.

Also informal and powerful indeed is the political process,

a process that is typically subterranean, below the surface, not discussed openly much less in formal meetings within the organization. By *political* I mean those activities and processes in an organization that emanate from self-interest, or the particular interest of a group, that may not be in the overall interest of the organization. When faced with the possibility of organizational change, organization members rarely ask at the outset, "What is the plan for the future?" but instead, whether openly or not, they ask, "How will the change affect me?"

It is not a matter of right versus wrong. It is more a simple matter of human nature. Thus, during the planning phase, it is imperative to address these "political" concerns, motivated by self-interest. That is, it is imperative to respond to the tacit question, "What's in it for me?" In answer are examples of the advantages to be provided by the future state:

- A mission and purpose that is more meaningful and inspiring
- A set of goals and objectives that are not only clearer but more sensible in potential for attainment as well
- A more participative, pleasant place to work
- A reward system that is more flexible and responsive to individual differences
- A more decentralized structure that supports greater worker autonomy as well as responsiveness to the customer
- A management information system that handles relevant, current, and therefore, useful data
- A set of management practices that engender trust

With such examples, a statement of the future can begin to be responsive to individuals' personal concerns. More specificity regarding such statements would be required, of course.

Summary

In planning changes, the first phase is unfreezing the organization. This means creating awareness of the need for change. This is best done by contrasting an actual with a more desired state. Also critical to this initial planning phase is leadership, in this case leadership capable of establishing conditions whereby the desired future state can be determined. And, finally, for adequate planning the political and power dynamics within the organization must be addressed. Addressing these organizational dynamics means involving informal leaders in the planning and making certain that the way the future state is described is responsive to organization members' inevitable question, "What's in it for me?"

Managing the Change Process

The toughest job is to *manage* the change process. In writing about this aspect of management, I can be logical, rational, and perhaps convey the idea that dealing with organizational change is indeed subject to management. In reality, however, managing change is sloppy — people never do exactly as we plan. And it follows Murphy's law — if anything can go wrong, it will. Moreover, organizational politics is always present, and change, after all, affects us all emotionally.

Even with these qualifications and the perspective that managing change is not always manageable, it is useful to consider certain principles and guidelines. The more a process may seem unmanageable, the closer we should stick to those activities that have been demonstrated to be helpful. The following principles and guidelines meet the criterion of demonstrated helpfulness.

Disengagement from the Past

Once it has been decided that change will happen and the planning has occurred, or is in process, time and energy need to be devoted to disengaging from the past, that is, from certain ways of working; from a program, project, or product; from a geographic location; or from a group of people with whom one previously worked. Disengagement may take a variety of forms. An event can be held to recognize in a formal way what a certain program that will no longer be implemented provided for the organization, and what those people who were involved personally contributed.

The event could be celebratory in nature, yet at the same time clearly demonstrate that the program would no longer be operational.

In an organization with which I am familiar, an event like the process described above actually occurred. A particular program was to be phased out to make way for a new and different one. In this case, the program had involved research and development on a rocket used by NASA and the air force that gradually became obsolete. Yet R&D was conducted with the rocket program all along the way as if it would always exist and be constantly improved. Due to changing rocketry technology, such was not to be, however. After almost twenty years with this program the engineers and technicians involved were to be reassigned or encouraged to retire early. Change came surely and swiftly for these rocket professionals. Before taking on a new program and having to acquire some new knowledge and learn new skills, senior management conducted a brief event, actually a ceremony. On the front lawn in front of the administration building a table draped in black cloth was the focal point. Underneath the cloth was a small replica of the old rocket. After the table was uncovered, certain senior managers made very brief speeches extolling the former program and the people who had contributed to it over the years. All drank a toast, and the rocket was then covered again, symbolically buried. The head of the organization then gave a short explanation of the new program (solar energy for propulsion in space) that was replacing the old. The entire event took less than thirty minutes. Accomplished with this event were two important outcomes: first, an unequivocal symbolic act demonstrated the end of the program, and, second, affirmative recognition was provided for those who had been involved.

While one may not need to conduct a funeral or demonstrate an ending quite as dramatically, two critical principles of managing change should be considered, both tied directly to human emotion. One is the principle of "unfinished business" and the other concerns appealing to rather than ignoring people's feelings of pride.

Unfinished Business. When something is not complete we humans tend to attempt some form of completion. A simple example from introductory psychology is when viewing a figure such as the following,

we "psychologically" close the gap and complete mentally what we believe to be a circle. Less simple, but based on the same principle, is the situation when, for example, we have an argument with someone that fairly soon stops for one reason or another short of resolution; one tends to continue the argument mentally even though the other party is no longer present. We spend mental and emotional energy in an attempt to finish, to resolve, to complete the argument. So it is with organizational change. When newness is thrust on organization members, replacing, say, former ways of doing things with no time to disengage and "finish the business" of the former way, they will spend energy trying to deal with the incompleteness. This energy may take the form of continuing simply to talk about the former ways, or criticizing the new ways as clearly imperfect, or even more resistantly, sabotaging the new ways. What is referred to as "resistance to change" often reflects energy devoted to closure attempts. Providing some way for organizational members to disengage, to finish the past, at least to some extent, helps them to focus on the change and the future.

I am not the first to relate this important human principle to organizational change. Nadler (1981), building on the theoretical writings of Lewin and the work of Beckhard and Harris (1977), discusses this disengagement process in his integration of a number of managing change principles. He categorizes managing change into three broad needs or challenges: 1) the need to motivate change (Nadler includes disengagement within this challenge); 2) the need to manage the transition, where he elaborates on Beckhard and Harris; and 3) the need to shape the political dynamics of change. My treatment of this managing change section reflects Nadler's thinking as well as others', for example, Tichy (1983) and Tichy and Devanna (1986).

Pride. Even though pride is among the seven deadly sins, it can be appealed to in a positive way. People who have worked in a particular job over a period of years typically build feelings of personal pride in what they do. Sometimes when change comes and people are told they must now do things differently, not their old jobs anymore, an implied message may be that what they used to do is now wrong or no longer worthwhile. Often the tendency on the part of management is to want to "get on with it" and quickly forget the past. We no longer need to manufacture that product, provide that service, and so on.

The point is that when change takes place and no time is given to recognize that even though an era has ended, what organizational members had been doing was worthwhile, they will tend to feel less worthwhile themselves. The stronger this feeling, the more organizational members' energy will be focused on dealing with their wounded pride. Usually a simple yet formal recognition that people had worked on important products or services for the organization and that significant contributions were made will be sufficient. This kind of act again helps organizational members to deal with potentially strong, human emotions, to achieve some degree of closure, and gradually to disengage from the past.

Managing the Transition

As Beckhard and Harris (1987) emphasize, creating a transition management team can be very important and useful to the change process. The larger and more complex the change effort, the more systematic, concentrated attention needs to be paid to the management process. An occasional committee or task force meeting may not do the job. It may be wise to appoint a full-time person to manage the transition with others assigned on a part-time basis. Large, complex change will not manage itself; that's the point. Other important factors to manage in the change process, as Nadler (1981) has highlighted, are the following:

Involvement. As noted before, a principle of behavior that is central to effective management, in general, and managing change, in particular, is "involvement leads to commitment." Stated a bit more elaborately, the degree to which people will be committed to an act is a function of the degree to which they have been involved in determining what that act will be.

For any given change goal, there will likely be multiple paths to that goal. Some of these paths may be more efficient than others, but most if not all paths that people can think of will lead to goal accomplishment. Due to circumstances leaders and managers of change may not always involve organizational members to any significant degree in establishing the primary goals. For purposes of gaining commitment, involving organization members in the planning of *how to reach* those goals is critical, however.

To repeat, there are usually different ways to reach a singular goal and one way is not always significantly different from a number of other ways. Thus, delegating decisions of implementation, that is, allowing organization members who must carry out the plans for reaching the goal to determine for themselves the plans or paths for getting there, will increase overall commitment to the change effort.

When possible it is beneficial, in order to gain commitment, to involve people in decisions that will directly affect them. At times, however, only a few executives will have the requisite information or relevant experience for optimizing the effectiveness of decisions regarding goals. Under these conditions, executives can carefully explain to organizational members the logic underlying a change decision and they will typically accept the change goal. To proceed then with telling them in detail about how to reach the goal is to risk resistance. The point is that executives can more easily win acceptance for a predetermined goal, provided the goal is viewed as challenging yet reasonable, than they can win acceptance of a predetermined implementation plan. Commitment, therefore, can be gained by involving organization members in the transition planning.

Multiple Leverage. Often managers of change rely too heavily on a singular system lever to move the organization toward the desired change. The lever most often chosen is structure. "Changing the organizational chart will do the job" is too frequently accepted as a valid assumption. In a study of successful versus unsuccessful OD efforts, Burke, Clark, and Koopman

(1984) found that the intervention most associated with lack of success was a change in the structure and that intervention was the only change made.

In large, complex organizations composed of many subsystems, when one of these subsystems is changed, eventually all other subsystems will be affected. This principle is based on sound, general system theory (Katz and Kahn, 1978). Therefore, when managing change multiple systems, or levers, must be considered. At the top of the list is strategy. A change in strategy best *precedes* structural change (Chandler, 1962). Moreover, when a structural change is made, changes in the management information system are likely to be required. Since it is also likely that different management practices will be needed, changes in the reward system to reinforce these new practices will help to ensure the overall success of the change effort.

The general idea to keep in mind, then, is the fact that organizations are dynamic, open systems. Changing an organization successfully requires that attention be paid to its multiplicity of subsystems, or levers, in tandem and in mutual support of the overall effort.

Feedback. In the face of ambiguity about how things are going, people more often than not assume the worst: "I knew this change wouldn't work!" To keep momentum, positive energy directed toward the change goal(s), providing feedback to organizational members about progress, regardless of how minor the progress may be, will help. Periodic progress reports, additional information incorporated within the management information system, conducting brief celebratory events when a change milestone is reached, are examples of how to monitor progress and, more important, ways to provide organizational members with relevant feedback.

Symbols and Language. To keep organization members focused and oriented, it is beneficial to have some symbol, acronym, or slogan to represent the change goal(s). The marketing department can be helpful with this process.

The principle is this: It is not always possible to state change goals in clear, simple statements. While a new organizational strategy or mission may be clear in the minds of senior management, since they have perhaps discussed and debated it for months and months, when put in writing, the new strategy may come across to the majority of people in the organization as vague, quite general, and abstract. Using a symbol may help not only to simplify and clarify the change goal but to capture organizational members' imagination and enthusiasm as well. A change in strategy from a technology-driven organization to a customer-driven one might, for example, be symbolized by a question inscribed on, say, a paperweight for each organizational member's desk or work area, which asks, "Have you talked with a customer today?"

An actual example, one with which I had some personal involvement, was created for a specific group within a large change effort at British Airways. The example concerned a training of trainers program for selected line managers. They were trained to help conduct a one-week residential Managing People First (MPF) program for upper-middle and middle management, well over 1000 managers in total. Although couched within a training of trainers objective, the large, broader objective was to indoctrinate sixteen hand-picked, high-potential managers with the underlying rationale for the specific MPF program and for the overall British Airways cultural change effort. Their broader mandate called for them to be change agents, to model the new behaviors associated with the desired culture. I referred to them as "culture carriers." They were to help leverage change. Our symbol for them was a lever with a hand gripping it and the accompanying slogan was the Greek philosopher Archimedes' famous quote, to paraphrase in English, "Give me a fulcrum [lever] and a place to stand, and I will move the world."

Stabilizing the Change

The stabilization process should begin during the disengagement stage. Just as important for organization members to learn about what will be different is to be informed about what will *not* change. During times of significant change, when people are clear about what is not changing, amid all that is, they have something stable to hold on to, an anchor. For example, even though an organization might be changing its strategy and structure, people could still be rewarded for their performance as before, say, on merit. If despite considerable change occurring, organizational members can count on their rewards being administered as before, knowledge of this element of stability will help them cope with the uncertainties. As a close friend once said to me years ago, "Never try to change everything at once."

A reward system is central to stabilizing change once it is underway. As new practices begin to occur, as people begin to behave in ways that help to move the organization toward the change goal(s), and as milestones are reached, the reward system should be deployed to reinforce these new, "right" behaviors and directions. As Tom Peters has put it, "Catch people doing the right thing."

Formally and publicly recognizing people for having helped to move the organization in the change direction will not only serve to reinforce and stabilize the new behaviors but will send a clear signal as well to others in the organization as to what the "right" behaviors are.

A final process of stabilizing the change, and clearly not mutually exclusive from the above points regarding the reward system, is to arrange for certain organization members to serve as "guardians" of the new way of doing things (Hornstein, Bunker, Burke, Gindes, and Lewicki, 1971). They serve primarily as role models, as "norm carriers" of the new culture. Provided these people are carefully selected and strategically placed in the organization, that is, they are seen as powerful leaders and representative of the future, they can help significantly to stabilize the change.

Summary

By way of summary, refer to Fig. 6–1. The model depicts the three broad phases of planning, managing, and stabilizing the change effort as well as the more specific activities recommended for each phase.

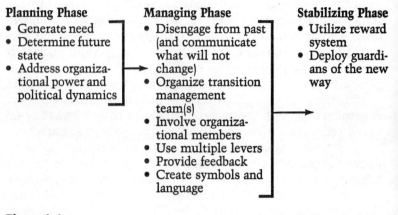

Figure 6–1
A Model for Managing Change

Measuring Progress of the Change Effort

How can you tell if you are making any progress in a change effort? My general answer to this question is, "Not in the most obvious ways." There are at least four ways to tell.

1. The quantity of problems that organization members must handle may not be any different. In the short run, however, the quantity may actually increase as people attempt to sort out which problems to tackle and how to deal with them. A clear sign of progress, in any case, is that the nature of problems has changed. Organization members are dealing with new and different problems. It is not a matter of problems having disappeared, it is a matter of different ones.

2. When organization members express frustration about a lack of progress regarding the change effort, as paradoxical as it may seem, such expression is a clear sign of progress. People are complaining about the right things. The following illustration should help to clarify this point.

Several decades ago Abraham Maslow spent a summer observing work in a high-technology company in Southern California. He kept a diary of his observations and later converted it into a book (Maslow, 1965). Among many of Maslow's observations one has always stood out for me, his distinction between grumbles and meta-grumbles. Grumbles are complaints about relatively small matters — "We never seem to have enough copy machines that are in good operating condition," "Why can't someone arrange for better maintenance of this building?" — are examples. In other words, the grumbles concern hygiene factors, to use Herzberg's term, those aspects of work life that contribute to one's level of dissatisfaction. Meta-grumbles, on the other hand, are complaints about such things as lack of clarity about goals, people needing to have more autonomy in carrying out their assignments, or expressing a desire for greater teamwork and collaboration. These complaints are about broader organizational concerns, usually beyond an individual matter. Maslow contended that managers should be happy to hear meta-grumbles, that underneath such complaining was motivation to be tapped and directed for the good of the overall organization.

So it is in assessing progress toward change. Meta-grumbles should be music to management's ears.

3. When issues, concerns, and progress reports regarding the change effort routinely become a part of the agenda for regular managers and staff meetings, that is a sign of progress. This means that the change effort is being monitored and constantly attended to.

4. And, finally, indicative of progress is when special events are held from time to time that assess progress, reevaluate the direction, celebrate milestones achieved, and recognize individuals for their accomplishments in helping with the change effort.

Summary

In this chapter we have considered the planning and management of change. The overall process is what OD practitioners refer to as the intervention phase. According to Argyris, an effective intervention is one that 1) provides *valid information* for the client organization, 2) allows for *choice* by the client regarding the specific steps to be taken, and 3) leads to *commitment* on the client's part to those action steps for change.

In planning change it is important, first, to assure that a need for change is determined if not developed, and second, to address the power and political dynamics of the organization. Managing the change effort is essentially transition management and concerns disengaging from the past, involving people in planning implementation, organizing a transition management team, using multiple leverages, providing feedback, and creating symbols and language to help focus the effort. The final phase, stabilizing the change, consists of utilizing the reward system to reinforce the new "ways of doing things" and putting into place key individuals to serve as "guardians" of the change goal(s).

Four ways to assess progress toward the change were covered. The four — different problems, meta-grumbles, change concerns as part of a regular meeting agenda, and progress review events — were described as not-so-obvious ways to determine progress.

7

Does OD Work?

Does OD work? This is the simplest of questions, but one of the most difficult to answer, at least definitively. Yet it is a critical question to address, especially so for the practice of OD in the United States. "Does it work?" is one of the first questions managers ask about anything new. In this chapter we shall therefore first respond to the question, but then quickly move to the caveats involved in attempting an answer. Next we shall consider obstacles to conducting an evaluation, the seventh phase of any OD effort, and finally we shall conclude by arguing the importance of evaluation regardless of the problems involved and the pressures against such an activity.

Does It Work?

When done according to the principles and practices expounded in this brief volume, my experience is that OD works. But my experience and others' experience in "successfully" practicing OD is not enough. So-called hard evidence is needed. And, indeed, there is some. French and Bell (1978), for example, selected nine studies that they considered supportive of OD's effectiveness:

1. "Breakthrough in Organization Development" (Blake, Mouton, Barnes, and Greiner, 1964)
2. *Management by Participation* (Marrow, Bowers, and Seashore, 1967)
3. "Short- and Long-Range Effects of Team Development Effort" (Beckhard and Lake, 1971)
4. "Eclectic Approach to Organizational Development" (Huse and Beer, 1971)
5. "Participative Decision Making: An Experimental Study in a Hospital" (Bragg and Andrews, 1973)
6. "OD Techniques and Their Results in 23 Organizations" (Bowers, 1973)
7. "Expectation Effects in Organizational Change" (King, 1974)
8. "Effects of Organizational Diagnosis and Intervention on Blue-Collar Blues" (Hautaluoma and Gavin, 1975)
9. "Organization Development and Change in Organizational Performance" (Kimberly and Nielsen, 1975)

Other studies could be included, such as the one by Golembiewski, Hilles, and Kagno (1974). So, there is evidence.

There are problems, however. From a survey of sixty-three organizations regarding their knowledge and use of organization development, Heisler (1975) found, among other things, that the major criticism of OD efforts was the difficulty in evaluating their effectiveness. A number of others have made similar observations; see, for example, King, Sherwood, and Manning (1978), Morrison (1978), Porras (1979), and Porras and Patterson (1979). We shall now consider the nature of some of these problems and issues.

Research Issues in Evaluating OD Efforts

The overriding issue in OD evaluation is purpose — whether the research effort is evaluation or knowledge generation, whether it is for the benefit of the client or the social scientist. Since the topic is *evaluation*, that should be the obvious concern, not scientific generation of knowledge; but the assessment methodology — how we collect and analyze our information for evaluative purposes — is based on the traditional scientific method. We control and manipulate some independent variables, make some interventions, and see if any difference occurs with respect to some dependent variables. We decide to use team building as an intervention, for example, and we collect information (dependent variable) to see if it made any difference. We might use a questionnaire to ask team members if they feel more satisfied with and committed to the team, and we might determine if the team's work performance increases after the team-building effort has occurred. Even if our data showed increased satisfaction, commitment, and work performance, it would be difficult to demonstrate that the team-building intervention has *caused* these outcomes unless we had also collected data from a matched control group, a similar team for which no team building had been done, and could compare data for the same period for the two groups. Another critical factor in this evaluation would be the people who collect and analyze the data. Numerous studies have shown that the researcher can effect the outcome (Rosenthal, 1976). This brings up the question of objectivity. To be scientific, or objective, the researcher should be someone other than the team-building consultant or the organization members involved.

Argyris (1970) has argued, however, that the more scientific the evaluation is, the less it is likely to be relevant to and therefore used by the client. He states that the traditional scientific methods of evaluation (his term is "mechanistic") "tend to create primarily dependent and submissive roles for the clients and provide them with little responsibility; therefore, the clients have low feelings of essentiality in the program (except when they fulfill the request of the professionals)" (Argyris, 1970: p. 105). To overcome these problems of evaluation research, Argyris argues that an organic approach is required, one that involves the client more directly in decisions about what data to collect and how to collect them.

If the research to be done is evaluative, and if the data are to be used by the client for further decision making, then the client should be involved in the research process itself, since this involvement will lead to more valid data and increased likelihood that the data will be used. This involvement is not scientific in the strict sense of the word, but our major concern and purpose is the collection and analysis of valid information. So-called scientific research in an organizational setting may generate invalid data (Argyris, 1968).

To be more specific, we shall now examine some primary research issues and problems associated with the evaluation of an organization development effort. The issues and problems are addressed in the form of six questions, which are not necessarily mutually exclusive.

1. What Is Organizational Effectiveness? In general, the goal of an OD effort is to improve the organization, to make it more effective, whether the effort is with a large, total system or with a division — a subsystem of a larger organization. It is not a simple matter to define effectiveness (Goodman and Pennings, 1980) or to get people to agree on a definition. Cameron (1980) points out that there are at least four different criteria for organizational effectiveness and that these criteria differ significantly from one organization to another. The differences are particularly apparent when comparing profit-making organizations with nonprofit organizations. The four criteria or models are as follows:

- *The goal model.* Organizational effectiveness is defined in terms of the extent to which the organization accomplishes its goals.
- *The system resource model.* Effectiveness is equated with the ability to acquire needed resources.
- *The process model.* Effectiveness is defined in terms of how smoothly the organization functions, especially the degree of absence of internal strain in the organization.
- *The strategic constituencies model.* Effectiveness is determined by the extent to which the organization satisfies all its strategic constituencies — special interest groups.

As Cameron notes, these models or definitions of effectiveness may be useful or inappropriate, depending on the type of organization and the public or market it tries to serve. The goal model may be best when organizational goals are clear and consensual; the system resource model when inputs are clearly tied to outputs; the process model when there is a clear connection between internal organizational processes and primary tasks; and the strategic constituencies model when external special interest groups have considerable influence on what the organization does or is supposed to do. Not all organizations fit neatly into one or more of these models, however. Cameron suggests, therefore, that evaluative researchers raise six critical questions. He contends that answers to these questions will help in determining the right criteria for evaluating an organization's effectiveness. Cameron's six critical questions for the organizational effectiveness researcher are as follows:

1. What domain of activity is the focus? Effectiveness in one domain may militate against effectiveness in another. A high degree of effectiveness in marketing, for example, could have negative consequences for manufacturing or R&D.

2. Which constituencies' points of view are being considered? Effectiveness for one group may be ineffectiveness for another. In a university, for example, effectiveness for students is excellent teaching and learning conditions. For the faculty who provide this excellence, however, the time required may decrease their research effort and thus militate against their effectiveness as scholars, yet another critical dimension of a university's effectiveness.

3. What level of analysis is to be used? Effectiveness on the individual or team level, for example, may produce ineffectiveness on the organizational level.

4. What time frame is to be used? Effectiveness criteria change over time; short-term and long-term effectiveness are not necessarily the same. Short-term criteria for business may be profits, but long-term criteria could be something else, such as becoming a multinational corporation, that might reduce short-term effectiveness.

5. What types of data are to be used? Organizational records may provide different results than perceptual data gathered from organization members or constituencies (Porras and Wilkens, 1980).

6. What referent is to be used? There are at least five available referents: comparative evaluations (Is the organization better than its competitors?); normative evaluations (Is the organization effective compared with some ideas model?); goal-centered evaluation (Did the organization reach its goals?); improvement evaluation (Did the organization improve over past performance?); and trait evaluation (Does the organization possess traits that are indicative of effective organizations?).

It should thus be apparent that determining organizational effectiveness is not simple. Obtaining answers to Cameron's six questions would certainly help.

2. *What Is OD in the Organization Development Effort?*
As illustrated in this book, OD is many things, and there are seven major phases in an OD effort. For evaluative research purposes, do we consider all these phases or just the intervention phase? Kahn (1974) stated accurately that at least in the scientific sense, OD is not even a concept: "It is not precisely defined; it is not reducible to specific, uniform, observable behaviors; it does not have a prescribed and verifiable place in a network of logically related concepts, a theory" (Kahn, 1974: p. 490). Different OD interventions will also result in different outcomes (Porras, 1979). For the practice of OD, the fact that the concept of OD lacks precision is not necessarily a problem unless we consider evaluation a part of the practice. In my opinion, evaluation is part of the practice, and we do indeed have a problem. Overcoming this problem involves being more precise. The more specific and precise we can be in defining the variety of activities coming under the rubric of OD, the more we will be in a position to evaluate the effectiveness of these activities. A way of increasing this precision is to achieve greater clarity about the remaining four questions.

3. *What Is the Independent Variable?* In an examination of thirty-eight research studies conducted on various aspects of OD, Pate, Nielsen, and Bacon (1977) reported that they had considerable difficulty in categorizing variables from the studies. They could not be sure whether the independent variable was the OD intervention itself or whether OD was only instrumental in the manipulation of some other independent variable. They took the view that OD is instrumental but does not constitute the independent variable as such. "For example, one might expect introduction of participative decision making (OD intervention) to facilitate worker awareness of the rationale for organizational actions (independent variable), which in turn may increase support and commitment to those actions (dependent variables) (Pate, Nielsen, and Bacon, 1977: pp. 450–51). Their emphasis of this issue is helpful because we can now be clearer about what activities to evaluate specifically. Perhaps one more example will be useful for clarifying this point. Suppose that, as a result of an OD diagnosis, a need for a new organizational structure is determined. Suppose further that a new structure is planned and implemented (OD intervention). This new structure changes authority relationships in that managers lower in the hierarchy now have more delegated authority for decision making. This changed relationship in authority would be the independent variable, and the differences in work performance, such as net profit and turnover, would be the dependent variables.

4. How Can We Control Variables? As organizations are dynamic systems, this is a question of causal attribution — determining whether the consequences of a change can be attributed to organization development. As noted earlier, the more we can control our research conditions (for example, by having a control condition or control group for comparison) the more we will be able to state with confidence what is cause and what is effect. In dynamic, changing organizations, however, this is almost impossible to do. It is difficult, for example, to persuade a manager to subject his or her organization to a series of time-consuming data-collection activities for the purpose of providing a control group. The manager is likely to ask, "What's in it for us?" It is even more difficult to find an appropriate control group. There are rarely two subsystems within an organization, much less two distinct organizations, that do the same things, have the same types of people, and are managed the same way.

With so much going on in the organizational world and with most of this array of activities being impossible to control, we have what Campbell and Stanley (1966) refer to as a problem of internal validity: determining whether what we did by way of change made a measurable difference. In the absence of pure control group conditions, the true experimental design for research purposes, Campbell and Stanley have provided what they call quasi-experimental designs. These designs, though not perfect from a research perspective, provide ways for controlling certain conditions so that validity will be enhanced. Their time-series design is a good example. In this design several measures are taken at certain intervals *before* the intervention and several measures are taken at essentially the same intervals *after* the intervention. They diagram this design as follows, where O is the observation (measurement) and X is the experimental treatment or intervention:

$$O_1O_2O_3O_4 \quad X \quad O_5O_6O_7O_8$$

If it can be shown 1) that there are no significant differences among the first four observations, O_1–O_4, 2) that there are significant changes from the first four to O_5, and 3) that there are then no significant differences among O_5–O_8, then the differences that occurred between O_1–O_4 and O_5–O_8 must be a result of X, not merely the passage of time or other variables. Berkowitz (1969) has elaborated on this design in the context of evaluating organization development. The Pate, Nielsen, and Bacon (1977) study showed that most evaluation studies had used a quasi-experimental design for evaluating OD efforts. Thus, Campbell and Stanley's work is highly relevant and useful for OD evaluation.

5. What Changed? Golembiewski, Billingsley, and Yeager (1976) drew distinctions among three types of change, which they labeled alpha, beta, and gamma. *Alpha* change concerns a difference that occurs along some relatively stable dimension of reality. This change is typically a comparative measure before and after an intervention. If comparative measures of trust among team members showed an increase after a team-building intervention, for example, then we might conclude that our OD intervention had made a difference. Golembiewski et al. assert that most OD evaluation research designs consist of such before-and-after self-reports.

Suppose, however, that a decrease in trust occurred, or no

change at all. One study has shown that, although no decrease in trust occurred, neither did a measurable increase occur as a consequence of team-building intervention (Friedlander, 1970). Change may have occurred, however. The difference may be what Golembiewski, Billingsley, and Yeager call a *beta* change, a recalibration of the intervals along some constant dimension of reality. As a result of team-building intervention, team members may view trust very differently. Their basis for judging the nature of trust changed, rather than their perception of a simple increase or decrease in trust along some stable continuum.

A *gamma* change "involves a redefinition or reconceptualization of some domain, a major change in the perspective or frame of reference within which phenomena are perceived and classified, in what is taken to be relevant in some slice of reality" (Golembiewski, Billingsley, and Yeager, 1976: p. 135). This involves change from one state to another. Staying with the example, after the intervention team members might conclude that trust was not a relevant variable in their team-building experience. They might believe that the gain in their clarity about roles and responsibilities was the relevant factor and that their improvement as a team had nothing to do with trust.

Thus, selecting the appropriate dependent variables, determining specifically what might change, is not as simple as it might appear. This is especially important when self-report data are used.

6. Who Will Conduct the Research and Who Will Use the Results? The last issue to be addressed is the people involved in the evaluation effort. To avoid the possibility of a Pygmalion effect and to increase the probability of objectivity, it is best that the researcher be someone other than the OD consultant. Both the researcher and the consultant are interveners into the organization, however, and therefore it is imperative that they collaborate. The researcher needs to know not only the consultant's overall strategy — change goals, targets, and so forth — and what interventions might be used, but also what the consultant's predictions are concerning what should change as a result of the OD effort. The researcher is both a data gatherer and analyzer and a consultant, in the sense that he or she must work directly and collaboratively with the client. In using Argyris's (1970) organic approach, the researcher involves the client in 1) defining research goals, 2) determining research methods and strategy, and 3) interpreting the results. Involving the client (the research subject) in the research effort requires many of the same skills and abilities needed by the OD consultant (see Chapter 8).

The people who will make decisions as a result of the evaluation research must be involved. These people may or may not be directly involved in the OD process itself, but the decision makers need to be involved by the researcher in much the same way that the organization members who are directly involved in the OD process would be participating in the research goals, methods, and interpretation. This involvement of the decision makers helps ensure that the research results will be valid and will be utilized for further decision making.

In addition to these issues in evaluating OD efforts and the inherent problems in doing so, there are a number of pressures against conducting this seventh phase of an OD effort in the first place. We shall now examine some of these more important obstacles.

Pressures Opposed to Evaluation

The evaluation process of OD practice can be compared to an annual physical examination — everyone agrees that it should be done, but no one, except a highly motivated researcher, wants to go to the trouble and expense of making it happen. We shall examine first some of the reasons for opposing evaluation and then conclude with reasons for going ahead with this phase.

At least four sets of people are involved in relation to OD evaluation: the manager or decision maker, the organization members who are directly involved in the OD process (the manager or decision maker may or may not be in this process), the OD consultant, and the evaluation researcher. There are pressures on each of these categories of people to ignore evaluation.

The Manager or Decision Maker. Managers want results. If interventions in an OD effort are accompanied by change in certain organizational areas that are important to managers — such as increased profits, decreased absenteeism, or increased morale — that is often all that is necessary for a manager to choose to continue with OD or to move on to other things. As Beer notes: "Unfortunately, managers typically assume that the effects of OD on these indices will be self-evident and they lose sight of the complexity of factors that might cause change in them" (1980: p. 246). Managers want to know *if* it works, not *why* it works. Such managers are usually found in fast-moving, marketing-oriented organizations, where short-term results are rewarded. There are other types of managers, however.

Managers in highly technical, scientific organizations may take the opposite stance. They may demand proof, hard empirical evidence, before they will decide. For these managers, a quasi-experimental design, with perceptual data as the mainstay, may strike them as soft, lacking in objectivity and scientific rigor. These managers might argue that, unless you can measure the consequences of an organization development effort in a rigorous, scientific manner, an evaluation is not worth doing. They might even argue that OD itself is not worthwhile, since so much is dependent on techniques that are nonscientific.

Opposition to evaluation research from managers who are in key decision-making roles may take either extreme: evaluation research is not necessary because the outcomes are self-evident or because the effects of OD cannot be measured scientifically. Other reasons for opposition from managers could be 1) the cost involved, 2) the amount of extra time it will take, or 3) the undesirability of an outsider coming in to do research on them.

The Organization Members Involved in the OD Effort. Opposition from those directly involved in the OD process may take the same forms as those mentioned with respect to the managers or decision makers. In addition to those possible if not highly potential forms of opposition, organization members may complain about the time it will take for them to answer the questionnaires, for example, when this time could be utilized more productively in getting on with further aspects of the OD effort. Stopping to fill out forms, to answer interview questions, or to document activities and events not only takes valuable time, but it may reduce the potential momentum of the change that is being attempted. They also might argue that the research staff is likely to be more beneficial to the goals of the researcher than to the goals of the organization's change effort.

The OD Consultant. The OD consultant is likely to want an evaluation study but for reasons that differ from those of the manager or decision maker. Managers are interested in OD's impact on outcomes — profits, turnover, costs, productivity — whereas OD consultants may be more interested in process —the impact that OD may have on behavior, attitudes, organizational procedures, changes in authority relationships, and the like. A study by Porras and Wilkens (1980) indicates that many OD consultants may be disappointed with evaluation research on organization development. Porras and Wilkens found that OD in a large organization had a positive impact on outcomes, such as unit performance, but a negative consequence for attitudinal and behavioral variables that described organizational and individual processes. As Porras and Wilkens noted, these latter, unexpected negative findings may reflect a beta change, not an alpha change (Golembiewski, Billingsley, and Yeager, 1976), since their measures of attitudes and behavior were through self-report questionnaires whereas their measures of unit performance came from company records.

The point here is not that OD consultants are uninterested in or opposed to determining OD's impact on outcomes but that certain factors may be more important to the consultant as a professional. According to Beer, "OD specialists are more interested in data that will help them intervene more effectively now and in the future" (1980: p. 246). Thus, with this potential difference in priorities, OD consultants and managers may consider one another opposed to evaluation research, when in reality they may only have different priorities or values about the goals of a research effort.

The Evaluation Researcher. The researcher is interested in both outcome and process measures, but his or her objectives for the use of the research results may differ from those of the other three groups of people concerned with an OD effort. The researcher is often more interested in contributing to the body of knowledge concerning organizations as changing systems or the effectiveness of organization development as a field than in providing information for the organization's decision makers. This difference in objectives or priorities can cause problems with planning and implementing an evaluation research effort, but opposition on the part of a researcher toward conducting an evaluation study is likely to occur for another reason. Most researchers are trained according to the traditional scientific method of research, which involves distancing oneself from and controlling the subjects of the research (client), not collaborating with them. Researchers are typically trained according to the mechanistic approach, whereas effective OD evaluation research calls for an organic approach.

Reasons for Conducting the Evaluation Phase

The forces that oppose evaluative research of an organization development effort are formidable and should not be dismissed lightly, but there are also compelling reasons for conducting evaluative research.

Briefly, the primary arguments for an evaluative research study of an OD effort are as follows:

1. An evaluation forces the definition of the change objectives.
2. An evaluation forces the clarification of the change outcomes that are expected.
3. An evaluation forces the clarification of how these change outcomes are to be measured.
4. An evaluation forces specificity with respect to how certain procedures, events, and activities will be implemented.
5. An evaluation helps to signal many of the problems and obstacles to be anticipated in the OD effort.
6. An evaluation facilitates planning for next steps and stages of organizational improvement and development.

As we know from system theory, particularly as applied to organizations, there may be no such thing as a single cause for a single effect. Systematic evaluation will provide many of the causal answers for what occurs and has occurred in organizations. Generally, but perhaps most important, evaluation forces clarity about what *effectiveness* is for an organization.

Finally, it is important to conduct *some* kind of evaluation rather than none at all. And rather than become embroiled in the issue of whether an outside researcher or the OD practitioner conducts the evaluation, and in the spirit of OD practice anyway, perhaps the OD practitioner can *facilitate* an evaluative process; help the client do the job themselves.

8

The OD Consultant

To be seen as a consultant is to have status, and thus many people aspire to the label and the role. A consultant is one who provides help, counsel, advice, and support, which implies that such a person is wiser than most people.

Although the label *consultant* usually conveys an image of one who provides help, there are obviously many different types of consultants. The purposes of this chapter are 1) to provide a context for the unique role and function of an OD consultant, 2) to consider the different roles and functions of an OD consultant, 3) to explore the kinds of personal characteristics that are needed for OD consultation and the types of people who are in the field, and 4) to suggest ways for those who want to become OD consultants to do so.

Context for Roles and Functions

There are various ways of considering an OD consultant's role. We shall consider first the places one may find an OD consultant; next we shall look at the consultant's role with a client and the multiple roles of OD consultants with one another; and then we shall examine the OD consultant's role as compared with other types of consultants or change agents. The purpose of this first section is to provide a context for understanding and clarifying the OD consultant's role. The next section will examine the specifics of the role itself.

Where OD Consultants Are Located

Organization development consultants are found either inside an organization, as full-time or part-time employees, or outside organizations, with those organizations considered as clients. Internal consultants are usually located within the human resources, personnel, or employee relations function; they may be part of an OD department and serve exclusively in an OD capacity; or they may combine OD consultation with other duties, such as training, counseling, research, or career assessment and development. Thus, internal OD consultants usually operate in a staff function, and they serve line managers throughout the organization.

External OD consultants may be employed by a consulting firm, may be self-employed, or may have academic appointments and consult only part of the time. In the past, external OD consultants usually came from colleges and universities. Now they are more likely to come from consulting firms or work on their own as full-time independent consultants.

Organization development consultants may serve managers or one another. The following diagram, suggested by Lundberg and Raia (1976) provides a quick picture of these different roles.

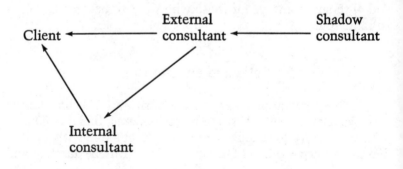

A shadow consultant (Schroder, 1974) serves as a sounding board, an advisor, and a confidant for the consultant who is working directly with a client. The external consultant may serve as a shadow consultant for the internal consultant or as a direct consultant to the client. If the organization employs more than one OD consultant, they can serve as shadow consultants to one another.

Comparisons of the OD Consultant with Other Types of Consultants

Edgar Schein (1969) contrasts the process consultant role (a primary but not exclusive role and function of an OD consultant) with the *purchase model* and the *doctor-patient model*. According to Schein, the purchase model is the most prevalent form of consultation, essentially consisting of the client's purchase of expert services information. A client's employment of a consultant to conduct a market research study is an example of purchasing both expert service and information. The doctor-patient model consists of the client's 1) telling the consultant what is wrong with the organization, usually in the form of symptoms ("Our turnover is too high." "We're losing market share with respect to product X." "Our management information system is a mess.") and then 2) expecting the consultant to prescribe a remedy for the problem.

Schein contrasts these two models with the process consultant, one who helps the client organization 1) diagnose its own strengths and weaknesses more effectively, 2) learn how to see organizational problems more clearly, and 3) share with the consultant the process of diagnosis and the generation of a remedy. Schein also states: "It is of prime importance that the process consultant be expert in how to *diagnose* and how to *establish effective helping relationships* with clients. Effective (process consultation) involves the passing on of both these skills" (1969: p. 8).

Thus the primary though not exclusive function of OD consultants is to help clients learn how to help themselves more effectively. Although consultants occasionally provide expert information and may sometimes prescribe a remedy, their more typical mode of operating is *facilitation*.

While a typical mode, facilitation is not the only function or role of OD consultants. The next section summarizes the array of consultant roles from which OD consultants may choose.

Roles and Functions

The Lippitt and Lippitt Model

Using a continuum from directive to nondirective, Lippitt and Lippitt (1975) have devised a descriptive model of eight different roles for a consultant. They do not use OD as their frame of reference but it is clearly implied, since their advocate role, the one closest to the directive end of the continuum, is within the context of helping and working with the client rather than in opposition, like the OP type from Tichy's (1974) research. By *directive*, Lippitt and Lippitt mean that the consultant's behavior assumes a leadership posture and that he or she initiates activities, whereas at the opposite extreme — nondirective — the consultant merely provides data for the client to use or not. All along the continuum the consultant is active; what varies is how directive or nondirective this activity becomes. Lippitt and Lippitt also note that these roles are not mutually exclusive. The consultant may, for example, serve as a trainer and educator and as an advocate at the same time. Figure 8–1 summarizes the Lippitt and Lippitt model, and the following are brief descriptions of the identified roles.

Advocate. In this role, the consultant attempts to influence the client. The advocacy may take either of two different forms: content advocacy, attempting to influence the client to select certain goals or to ascribe to particular values — or methodological advocacy — attempting to influence the client to use certain methods of problem solving or change management.

Technical Specialist. In this role, the consultant provides a particular expertise. Again, the form could either be content, such as providing information about how to compose work groups for a particular task or about the effectiveness and validity of as-

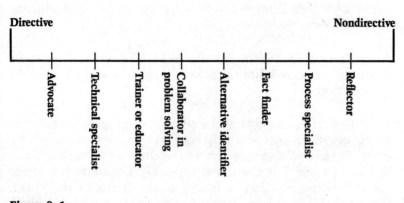

Figure 8–1
Eight Consultant Roles

Source: Adapted from G. L. Lippitt and R. Lippitt, *Consulting Process in Action.* San Diego: University Associates, 1978. Used with permission.

sessment centers, or methodological, such as designing an off-site meeting.

Trainer or Educator. An OD consultant is frequently cast in the role of teacher or manager and implementer of some learning activity. It is imperative that the OD consultant know about the process of adult learning and about designing and conducting learning activities.

Collaborator in Problem Solving. In this role, the consultant helps the client 1) to discern problem symptoms from problem causes, 2) to generate alternative solutions, and 3) to plan and implement corrective action steps. In general, the consultant raises many questions and issues, so that useful working data are generated, and joins the client in the decision-making process.

Alternative Identifier. In this role, the consultant performs all the activities associated with the previous role but does not collaborate with the client in making decisions.

Fact Finder. The consultant in this role is essentially serving as researcher, through interviewing, observing, or conducting a questionnaire survey.

Process Specialist. For this role, Lippitt and Lippitt describe the same activities as Schein (1969) describes for process consultation.

Reflector. The role of the consultant as reflector involves asking questions that will help clarify or perhaps change a situation. The consultant may serve as facilitator or catalyst for action in this role, but the action is merely a consequence of the questioning process and is totally in the hands of the client. Harvey (1977) describes this role as using the Socratic method. He provides a description of the role within the context of helping a client manage agreement (1977: ch. 14), and he explains the method with a case illustration. The label *reflector* or *Socratic* may imply a passive role, but the opposite is true. The consultant not only is active but may also be very confrontive, depending on the types of questions asked. Harvey states that the function of the Socratic consultant is

> (1) to help the individual (client) articulate the reality-based solution s/he would like to pursue; (2) to help the individual assess the potential reality of the fantasies which are preventing his/her taking action; (3) to recognize the individual's fear of separation (e.g., getting fired); (4) to recognize the need for connection as partial protection from the real stress that inevitably accompanies separation; (5) to help the individual face the reality that despite his/her planning and intentions s/he may make a choice which results in an outcome s/he may not like (getting fired); and (6) to assist the individual in becoming committed to living with the consequences whatever decision s/he may make. (1977: pp. 183–84)

Summary. The eight roles that Lippitt and Lippitt have identified are not the only roles and, as noted earlier, they overlap in that a consultant may be serving in one or more of the roles simultaneously or may be acting as an advocate one moment and as a reflector in another. Their model, though fairly simple and straightforward, nevertheless helps us to become clearer about 1) the multiple roles in which an OD consultant may function and 2) the situations in which one of these roles will serve better than others.

Marginality

Margulies (1978) has described the consultant's role differently and more generically. He argues that the OD consultant role is a marginal one. *Marginal* implies in between or on the edge — the periphery — and, accordingly, another term that Margulies uses is *boundary*.

First, Margulies contrasts two models of consulting with which we are already familiar: the *technical* consulting model and the *process* consulting model. His technical consulting model is like Schein's purchase and doctor-patient models and like Lippitt and Lippitt's technical specialist role, and his process model is the same as Schein's process consultation model. Margulies makes an analogy of technical-process with rational-intuitive and with the idea of the two-sided person represented by the two hemispheres of the brain. The OD consultant's role, he argues, is to function between these two halves, in the margin, being neither too technically oriented nor too process-oriented. Both sets of consultant expertise are appropriate, but for the OD consultant neither should be emphasized to the exclusion of the other. The consultant operates within the boundary of these two models of consultation, totally endorsing neither yet accepting both.

Margulies includes two other boundaries: the activities boundary and the membership boundary. For both, the OD consultant should operate at the boundary, in a marginal capacity. With respect to change activities, particularly implementation, the consultant must help but not be directly involved. Suppose, for example, an off-site team-building session for a manager and his subordinates was forthcoming. The consultant would help the manager with the design and process of the meeting but would not lead the meeting.

With respect to membership, the OD consultant is never quite in nor quite out. Although the consultant must be involved, he or she cannot be a member of the client organization. Being a member means that there is vested interest, a relative lack of objectivity. Being totally removed, however, means that the consultant cannot sense, cannot be empathetic, and cannot use his or her own feelings as data for understanding the client organization more thoroughly. Being marginal with respect to membership means that the consultant becomes involved enough to understand client members' feelings and perceptions yet distant enough to be able to see these feelings and perceptions for what they are — someone else's — rather than as an extension of oneself.

Being marginal is critical for both an external consultant and an internal consultant. The major concern regarding the internal OD consultant's role is that he or she can never be a consultant to his or her own group. If the group is an OD department, a member of this department, no matter how skilled, cannot be an effective consultant to it. It is also difficult for an internal OD practitioner to be a consultant to any group that is within the same vertical path or chain of the managerial hierarchy as he or she may be. Since the OD function is often a part of corporate personnel or the human resource function, it would be difficult for the internal OD consultant to play a marginal role in consulting with any of the groups within this corporate function, because the consultant would be a primary organization member of that function. Consulting with marketing, R&D, or manufacturing within one's organization, for example, would be far more feasible and appropriate, since the OD consultant could more easily maintain a marginal role.

It is understandable that an OD consultant's role can be a lonely one. The role can also create anxiety about one's accuracy of perception (no one to check it with but the client) and about one's choice of intervention (whether it is the right thing for the moment). Joining in fully, being a member, helps alleviate this loneliness and anxiety. Staying removed, distant, and aloof can also relieve the anxiety, since feelings are not involved. Doing either, however, lessens one's effectiveness as a consultant significantly. An obvious way to alleviate the problems of loneliness and anxiety is to co-consult. Working as an external and internal consultant team is probably the best way.

Abilities and Needs

The abilities an OD consultant needs to be effective are not so much specific skills but rather certain personal characteristics that can be used in a flexible manner.

Beer (1980) lists five role and personal characteristics that he considers important for the OD consultant:

1. *Generalists and specialist.* The OD consultant "is generalist in his organizational administrative perspective and a specialist in the process of organizational diagnosis and intervention" (Beer, 1980: p. 222).
2. *Integrator.* The OD consultant sees to it that key linkages are made between the client and needed resources, such as calling in a particular expert for a specific change objective, and between various subsystems within the client organization, particularly between top management and certain staff groups, such as those involved in planning and human resource management.
3. *Neutrality.* The OD consultant should have no career authority over members of the client organization, should have no particular ax to grind with respect to the solution of organizational problems, should have no desire to obtain a high position within the client organization, and should be neutral with respect to the organization's internal politics.
4. *Credibility.* The more OD consultants can demonstrate that they have knowledge of the organization and its functioning and the more they are associated with organizational successes rather than failures, the higher their credibility will be. As Franklin (1976) has shown, credibility is a significant variable linked to OD success.
5. *Marginality.* Here Beer cites Margulies and supports the argument for a boundary role for the OD consultant.

Consultants' Abilities

As Beer (1980) notes, these roles are difficult to maintain, requiring people with considerable ability. We shall now examine what some of these required abilities are. I consider that ten primary abilities are key to an OD consultant's effectiveness. Most of these abilities can be learned, but because of individual differences in personality or basic temperament, some of them would be easier for some people to learn than for others. The effective consultant should have the following abilities:

- The ability to *tolerate ambiguity*. Every organization is different, and what worked before may not work now; every OD effort starts from scratch, and it is best to enter with few preconceived notions other than with the general characteristics that we know about social systems.
- The ability to *influence*. Unless the OD consultant enjoys power and has some talent for persuasion, he or she is likely to succeed in only minor ways in OD. We will consider this point in more detail later.
- The ability to *confront difficult issues*. Much of OD work consists of exposing issues that organization members are reluctant to face.
- The ability to *support and nurture others*. This ability is particularly important in times of conflict and stress; it is also critical just before and during a manager's first experience with team building.
- The ability to *listen well and empathize*. This is especially important during interviews, in conflict situations, and when client stress is high.
- The ability to *recognize one's own feelings and intuitions quickly*. It is important to be able to distinguish one's own sensations from those of the client and also be able to use these feelings and intuitions as interventions when appropriate and timely.
- The ability to *conceptualize*. It is necessary to think and express in understandable words certain relationships, such as the cause-effect and if-then linkages that exist within the systemic context of the client organization.
- The ability to *discover and mobilize human energy*, both

within oneself and within the client organization. There is energy in resistance, for example, and the consultant's interventions are likely to be most effective when they tap existing energy within the organization and provide direction for the productive use of the energy.

• The ability to *teach* or create learning opportunities. This ability should not be reserved for classroom activities but should be utilized on the job, during meetings, and within the mainstream of the overall change effort.

• The ability to *maintain a sense of humor*, both on the client's behalf and to help sustain perspective. Humor can be useful for reducing tension. It is also useful for the consultant to be able to laugh at himself or herself; not taking oneself too seriously is critical for maintaining perspective about an OD effort, especially since nothing ever goes exactly according to plan, even though OD is supposed to be a *planned* change effort.

In addition to these abilities, it is important, of course, for the OD consultant to have self-confidence and to be interpersonally competent (Argyris, 1970). Finally, I think it is helpful for the consultant to have a sense of mission about his or her work as an OD practitioner. I do not mean to imply that OD consultants should be zealots, but rather that they should believe that what they are doing is worthwhile and potentially helpful to others. This belief helps to sustain energy, to lessen feelings of loneliness and anxiety, and it provides a reason for continuing to work on organizations that appear recalcitrant and impossible to change.

Consultants' Needs

Regardless of their abilities, OD consultants have personal needs. Like most people, we want to be competent and to be recognized for this competence. Although we may not be interested in winning popularity contests, we do not wish to be disliked. We like to achieve and we like to help. We also like to influence and we are attracted to power. We often face the dilemma, however, of wanting to facilitate and help and at the same time wanting to influence, to exercise power, and perhaps even to lead. Reconciling and integrating these often conflicting needs is very difficult. Exacerbating this dilemma is the probability that most people who are attracted to and who are currently in the field of organization development, as well as other consultants, are individuals who have a higher than average need for power.

Being aware of our needs, particularly with respect to power, should help us as consultants to be wary of our motives, but this awareness also will help us learn how to meet our needs and serve the client effectively.

Becoming an OD Consultant

I have been asked occasionally how one becomes an OD consultant. I have typically responded with such vague answers as "Well, it depends," since the question is difficult. There simply is no clear and systematic career path for becoming an OD consultant. Experienced people in the field may suggest such paths as going to a training laboratory, taking some psychology courses, tagging along with an experienced consultant to learn by observing and gradually trying some consulting interventions, reading some books, or attending the National Training Laboratories Program for Specialists in Organization Development. In the next few paragraphs I will attempt to answer the question of how one becomes an OD consultant a little more systematically.

Like any other field that consists of applying skills and implementing a particular kind of practice, experience is the best teacher for OD practice — or rather, experience accompanied by related feedback is the best teacher. One can have numerous experiences, but unless one receives feedback about which experiences are more related to effective practice, then learning rarely occurs. Thus, one should try to obtain experience in and feedback on consultative activities.

The second best way to become an OD consultant is by some combination of academic learning and nonacademic training.

Academic Training

A number of universities offer a curriculum either in organization development or in related courses. I suggest the following twelve courses, mostly at the graduate level, that will provide a good background for OD practice. These courses are fairly common, perhaps not all in a single university, but similar courses may be available. Obtaining education in these twelve subjects would be most useful:

1. *Organizational psychology* or organizational behavior. The former is typically offered in a department of psychology, the latter in a school of business or management. Either course provides the necessary background for understanding human behavior in an organizational context.
2. *Group dynamics.* This kind of course is a must. Organizations are composed of subsystems, usually in the form of work groups or managerial teams. Understanding the theory, research, and conceptual aspects of group behavior as well as the applicability of this knowledge helps one understand the utility of groups in organizations.
3. *Research methods.* Field research methods are preferable since they are the most applicable for learning about data collection and analysis in organizations.
4. *Adult learning.* This type of course is useful for understanding how organization members may learn from their experiences on the job as well as for knowing more about the appropriate rationale for designing training programs.
5. *Career development.* Since OD consultants are frequently involved in designing career development programs and are involved in human resource planning, background in this subject area is important.
6. *Counseling and interviewing.* This kind of course can provide critical skills, not only for diagnosis in general but also for specific help to individual organization members.
7. *Organization development.* Many universities now offer a one-semester or even a two-semester course in OD. The course may not be called OD, so one may have to read course descriptions carefully to find the right one.

8. *Training and development.* This type of course provides useful information about design of programs and about how to conduct certain learning activities.

9. *Action research and consultation.* This course may be the OD course. It usually offers good experience in data collection for diagnosis, feedback, and planned change. If the specific skills associated with this aspect of consultation are also included, so much the better.

10. *Human resource management.* This course, usually offered in a school of management or business, provides the necessary grounding in the organizational function that is most related to OD.

11. *Process consultation.* A course with this title is not likely to be available, but any course that provides an understanding of what process is and experience in dealing with it, the consultant aspects, should help. To clarify:

> The process consultant seeks to give the client "insight" into what is going on around him, within him, and between him and other people. The events to be observed and learned from are primarily the various human actions which occur in the normal flow of work, in the conduct of meetings, and in formal or informal encounters between members of the organization. Of particular relevance are the client's own actions and their impact on other people. (Schein, 1969: p. 9)

Looking for a course that would provide what Schein describes is the point. It would be even better if the course also included some substance and practice on interpersonal and intergroup conflict.

12. *Organization theory.* This course should follow the basic course on organizational behavior or organizational psychology. Usually this kind of course helps one learn about organizational design, effectiveness (performance criteria), and the organization as a system.

I purposely limited myself to twelve courses, conforming to a typical master's degree program requiring thirty-six to forty credits. Pepperdine University's nonresidential master of science in organization development program is an example, although their curriculum and what I have outlined are not exactly the same. The twelve courses I have listed assume that one would already have an undergraduate degree in psychology, sociology, or anthropology.

Nonacademic Training

Several professional development programs are offered by training organizations or by the continuing education divisions of universities. These provide useful training in both the knowledge and the skill appropriate to OD practice, but the weight is usually on the side of skill development. The following are ten avenues or programs for developing oneself toward becoming an OD practitioner:

1. *Basic laboratory training program.* This involves attending at least a five-day event devoted to improving one's interpersonal competence — a T-group, Gestalt group, a Tavistock group, or something very similar.
2. *Personal growth laboratory.* The first program listed emphasizes interpersonal development, whereas this one focuses on intrapersonal understanding. Since the primary instrument in OD work is the consultant practitioner, it is important that one know this instrument as well as possible.
3. *Training Theory and Practice.* This is the name of a program offered by the National Training Laboratories (NTL) Institute, and other organizations may offer a similar program. Attending such a program will provide an opportunity to learn about the design of training laboratories and the necessary skills for conducting them.
4. *Consultation skills.* Practice in consulting is imperative, and this type of program is ideal since it offers a safe environment for testing untried skills.
5. *Organization development laboratory.* This program

usually provides an introduction to the field and may range from a one-week version to a four-week one. Universities such as UCLA and the University of Michigan offer one-week programs; Teachers College, Columbia University, offers a two-week program; and organizations such as University Associates and the NTL Institute offer even more variety.

6. *Team-building programs.* Organizations such as the University of Michigan and Block–Petrella Associates offer training in how to consult with teams.

7. *Supervised experience.* Sometimes such an experience is provided as part of a consultation skills training program; otherwise, one needs to consult with an actual client and arrange some form of supervision from an experienced OD consultant. Having a mentor is a related avenue for professional and personal development.

8. *Internal consultant in a large organization.* An excellent way to get started in OD is to work for an organization that has an internal OD service for its managers. I emphasize *large* organization because the opportunities would be greater and more varied. One may not be able to join an internal OD group immediately, so the entry job should be at least closely associated with OD work, such as training, career development, or human resource planning. One can then make contacts, express interest, and arrange for an experience such as that suggested in number 7.

9. *Professional associations.* Belonging to and attending the meetings of certain associations devoted to OD can of course help one learn about and keep up with the field. Such organizations are the OD Network, the OD divisions of the American Society for Training and Development and the Academy of Management, and certain regional groups, such as those in New York, Philadelphia, Ohio, and the Bay Area in northern California.

10. *Advanced programs* for professional development. Programs such as the jointly sponsored Teachers Col-

lege, Columbia University and the University of Michigan's "Advanced Program in Organization Development and Human Resource Management" and Harvard's "Managing Organization Effectiveness" are designed for experienced OD practitioners and provide an opportunity for more advanced development.

Being an OD consultant means being a practitioner. We practice OD much as lawyers and physicians practice law and medicine, but there are no schools of organization development, no bar or boards to pass, and no licensing procedure. For a consideration of such matters, see Jones (1980). Certified Consultants, Inc. (formerly known as the International Association of Applied Social Scientists) and the OD Institute accredit OD consultants — but there is no systematic procedure or plan provided for how to become an OD specialist. Short of such a procedure or plan, I believe that some combination of academic training and professional development is the next best approach to becoming an OD consultant.

Part of the excitement of being involved in organization development is that, as a field, it is not all "put together" or "cut and dried." A new person coming into OD can still influence the shape, the form, and the eventual synthesis the field may take in the future. Since many OD people have higher-than-average needs to influence, and since many of us tend to distrust if not rebel against too much authority, perhaps the fact that the field of OD is still in an emergent phase is healthy (Burke, 1976; Friedlander, 1976). Opportunity still abounds.

Summary

In this chapter we have considered the role and personal characteristics of the OD consultant. The OD consultant may behave in a directive manner, perhaps even as an advocate, or, at the opposite extreme, may behave very nondirectively, serving perhaps as a reflector, primarily raising questions. For the most part, however, the OD consultant serves in a facilitative capacity, helping clients learn how to solve their own problems more effectively.

We also considered the role of the OD consultant from another perspective. Remaining marginal, at the boundary or interface between individuals, especially bosses and subordinates, and between groups and subsystems, is critical to effective consultation, at least from the vantage point of organization development practice. In this marginal role, the consultant functions in an organic way, attempting to intervene in a timely manner and according to what the client needs at the time. Consulting organically means that the practitioner must use himself or herself as an instrument, sensing client need by paying attention not only to what may be observed but also to his or her own feelings and intuitions. This form of consultation is not easy and is highly dependent on the skills of the consultant and subject to bias according to the consultant's personal values and attitudes. Obviously, the effective OD consultant will be sensitive to these issues.

9

Organization Development Now and in the Future

Recently I spent a day in a large manufacturing corporation exploring potential ways of translating a set of corporate values into daily behavior, especially on the part of the top 1000 managers. We were dealing with large-scale change in organizational behavior. During one of the breaks in our meeting an individual member of our group, with tongue in cheek, said to me, "I would be resistant to change if I only knew what to resist."

I was amused by the statement and, at the same time, struck by how the individual's comment was indeed a commentary. This corporation in the previous two years had undergone an incredible number of changes, with more to come. The company has experienced during the latter half of the 1980s more change than most large, billion-dollar corporations in the United States, yet when this corporation is compared with many others like it, the difference is only a matter of degree.

With so much change occurring and with the rate increasing geometrically, our notion of "resistance to change" and our ideas and beliefs about change are no doubt undergoing change. My client's expression of "not knowing what to resist," taken seriously, might mean for him a question of integrity and a question of energy. In the process of attempting to cope with so much change he might ask, "What should I choose to support or to challenge in an open, honest way?" "Where should I focus my energy, when it is clear that I am not able to deal with everything?"

For the individual, life is clearly more dynamic than it was a few decades ago. From an organizational change perspective, what may seem to be resistance more accurately might be, instead, quandary. The broader point to be made here is that where there is individual or group resistance there is energy and, for effective organizational change, it is a matter of orienting or redirecting that energy. Far worse than resistance, therefore, is apathy. It is rather difficult to orient or direct apathy.

The additional point of my statements so far, and more pertinent to this final chapter, is the fact that OD as a field has a bright future, *bright* meaning that OD is synonymous with change and change in organizational life is more of a constant than ever before. Anyone today who is reasonably competent in the practice of OD is not likely to be out of work in the foreseeable future.

To be more specific about OD now and in the future, I will consider the field according to three categories of practice: 1) strategic implementation and culture change, 2) new applications of OD, and 3) relationships and interfaces, or "Who is the client?"

Implementing Strategy and Culture Change

One way to understand something is to consider what it is not. The practice of OD is not what the more traditional management consulting firms do. A McKinsey, Booz Allen and Hamilton, or Arthur D. Little typically provide help to organizations that is technical, business, and economic in nature. As a rule, they do not provide consulting services in the people domain. In other words, they give recommendations and advice for changes that management should consider. These recommended changes may be in the organization's technology or business strategy, or both. These management consultants may suggest further to the client ways of implementing these changes. But they rarely provide help to the client in actually carrying out the recommendations for change. This stage is often the time when OD practitioners are brought in, that is, to help facilitate the change that has been recommended.

With respect to how people view OD practice today, compared with perceptions in the 1960s, two things have changed. First, OD is rarely seen as a "warm, fuzzy" way of dealing with people that is unrelated to the daily realities of organizational life and business objectives. Second, the practice of OD is now being perceived as a highly useful process of change implementation. OD has a critical part to play in the organizational change arena.

More specifically, and as noted in Chapter 6, planning a new strategy is one thing, implementing that new strategy is quite another. What has become clear to people involved in a fairly significant change in an organization's strategy, or even more complicated, its mission, is the fact that an organization's culture usually has to be changed for the new strategy to work successfully. I do not mean to imply that strategy and culture are mutually exclusive. After all, strategic decisions are made by executives within the context of their organizational culture, that is, based on their beliefs and assumptions. The point is that strategy changes are often decided "out of context" without due consideration of the culture. It is difficult if not impossible to implement a new strategy if the *way* of implementing decisions remains the same. That *way* of process is part and parcel to organizational culture and is the primary domain of organization development. Thanks to Peters and Waterman (1982), Deal and Kennedy (1982), and Schein (1985) management today readily accepts the idea that an organization, like a nation or society, has a culture, or the more the organization represents a conglomerate we should more accurately say that it has multicultures; culture, nevertheless.

More than ever, then, and even more so for the future, OD practitioners are involved in culture change, particularly when the need for such change is preceded by a management decision to seek new ways of doing business.

New Applications

Very little "new OD" has been created during the latter half of the 1970s and the 1980s. Team building no doubt still remains as the most common practice of OD consultants, which currently typically takes the form of "facilitating an off-site meeting." What is new, however, is 1) the application of organization development in organizations that have not as a rule used this form of consulting, for example, organizations involved in health care, 2) the provision of training in OD consulting skills for people other than those from the behavioral sciences or in the human resource domain, for example, information management and systems people, and line managers, and 3) the use of more sophisticated analytical methods to interpret questionnaire, survey data.

With respect to use of OD in organizations where there has been no precedence, health care systems, in particular, are being attracted to OD because they are undergoing such significant changes. Many of these are hospitals, which are making the transition from nonprofit institutions to profit-oriented businesses. As most people know, health care in the United States is undergoing sweeping changes. Competent OD practitioners are in a position to help considerably with these organizational changes. Other organizations that have not utilized OD but are likely to be attracted to its use more in the future are those that are changing from a highly regulated business, such as airlines, or a government-owned organization to an unregulated business or publicly owned organization, Jaguar of the United Kingdom being an example of the latter type of organization.

Regarding training others in OD consulting skills, it is likely that OD practitioners will become more involved in training others in what they do. Others in this case are corporate staff specialists, such as information management and systems experts, who heretofore have legislated to operational people what they can and cannot do but now are expected to serve rather than dictate. Having had personal experience in helping to train information management people in consulting skills, they represent a prototype of this new application of OD. The change that has occurred for these specialists is the growing sophistication on the part of line, operational people about computer and data processing. They know more than was true a decade ago about what their information needs are and what they want in response to their needs. Their expectation, therefore, is that the information management specialist will facilitate their obtaining what they want rather than determining it. The same kind of change regarding the role of staff specialists is true for planning experts, market researchers, and training directors. There are no doubt other examples. The point is that with a combination of line, operational people ("clients") becoming more knowledgeable about the expertise staff specialists provide and staff specialists become more vulnerable to reductions in force, that is, the trend toward smaller corporate staffs (see the predictions covered by Tom Peters (1987) referred to in Chapter 1), these staff specialists must modify their roles. Becoming more consultative and facilitative is a modification in the right direction. OD practitioners can indeed help.

And with respect to using more sophisticated methods to analyze questionnaire data, OD practitioners will be using, or clearly will *need* to be using, more powerful analytical tools to remain effective in the future, the use of computers and statistics other than merely averages and percentages in order to help clients understand more thoroughly the complexities, subtle nuances, and potential implications of organizational behavior. This type of application in OD, that is, gathering and analyzing data from numerous sources, is particularly pertinent to large, multicultural organizations where information from one segment explains very little about the total system. For an example of such analytical methods used in an OD context, see Bernstein and Burke (1987).

Relationships and Interfaces, or Who Is the Client?*

The point of this third category of OD practice, which is considerably larger than the previous two, is twofold: 1) to emphasize a bias of mine about how OD practitioners should conceive their practice, who the client really is, and 2) to highlight

*Based on an article written for the *OD Practitioner*: W. Warner Burke, "Who Is the Client? A Different Perspective," from *OD Practitioner*, vol. 14, No. 1, June 1982. By permission.

the area of OD consulting that is becoming more critical for the future practice of organization development, that is, relationships and interfaces.

I believe that the client in OD consultation is never one individual, regardless of position or role, or any particular group, team, or subsystem of the organization, or any combination thereof. Even though I generally subscribe to the idea of OD being "total system," I have trouble defining what the total system is since each one resides within yet a larger "total system."

Thus, I have come to think of my client as the *relationship* or *interface between* individuals and units within and related to the overall system. The arrows in Fig. 9–1 depict this idea of who the true client is. This *in-betweenness* is therefore the main scene of action of OD consulting practice.

From the perspective of the consultant role, this notion of client is not new. Argyris (1970) avoided terms such as consultant, change agent, or practitioner, favoring instead "intervenor" and "interventionist." These terms were, of course, an extension of his definition of a consultant intervention: "To intervene is to enter into an ongoing system of relationship, to come between or among persons, groups, or objects for the purpose of helping them" (Argyris, 1970: p. 115). For Argyris, then, to consult is to intervene.

Margulies characterized the role of the OD consultant as a marginal one (see Chapter 8). He argued that the degree to which the consultant is effective is a function of how capable he or she is 1) at maintaining a certain social distance between self and other individuals in the client organization and 2) at operating on the boundaries of units rather than exclusively within them. In these ways, the consultant can more readily maintain an objective stance *in between* persons and units in conflict rather than by being *with* one or the other.

While I agree with both Argyris and Margulies regarding the consultant role, I am here focusing on the other side, the client, and on the perspective of defining the client as relationships and interfaces rather than individuals and units, singular entities within the organization. To pursue this perspective, we shall first consider theory and then practice — the why and then the where and how. And, finally, we shall consider these opinions of mine for the future.

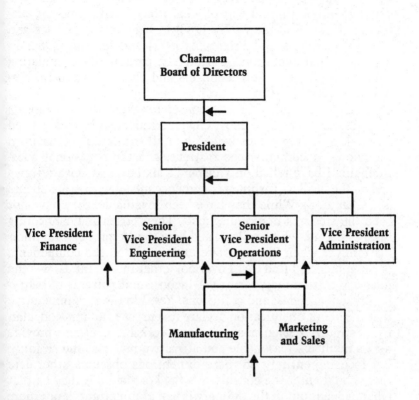

Figure 9–1
*Example of a Typical Functional Organizational Structure
(The arrows represent the arena of organization development
consultation.)*

Theory

General systems theory and theory that underlies Gestalt
therapy have both furnished me with useful conceptual frameworks for understanding OD practice (Burke, 1980). Notions of
entropy, input-throughout-output, and equilibrium from the former and the ideas of energy, existentialism, and polarities from
the latter have been particularly helpful to me in understanding
some mistakes I have made in consultation, that is, why some

efforts turned out other than as I had expected. Although I understand only a limited part of what I have read, I find the theoretical ideas of Capra (1977, 1983) in high-energy physics and Prigogine (Nicolis and Prigogine, 1977) and Jantsch (1980) in chemistry and evolution, respectively, particularly stimulating since their thinking both confirms and challenges general systems and related theory.

Capra stimulated me to consider organizational diagnosis in quite new ways. Like most OD practitioners, I have depended on models to help me make sense of all the data I collect from interviews, documents, observations, and the occasional questionnaire. I have relied on Weisbord's six boxes at certain times and on the Nadler–Tushman congruence model with other clients (see Chapter 5). While they have been invaluable, they have not been the sine qua non of diagnosis. Their boxes and connecting lines direct me where to look and how to interpret certain information, yet when I concentrate exclusively on the components of these models I find that I overlook other important data — the nuances, certain reappearing yet inconsistent patterns of behavior, hidden agendas, and collusions. Yes, I know it is imperative that the client organization declare its purpose and mission, clarify its strategy, design an appropriate, workable structure, provide for its members reasonable and attractive rewards, and so forth. But focusing entirely on these dimensions obscures other data that should enter the consultant's field of vision. It may be that what happens out of the ordinary is just as important, if not more so, than what happens routinely. It may be that repercussions in one or more of the boxes brought about by events in another box in the model are more important for diagnosis than what happens in the changed box itself. For example, a change of leadership may have stronger implications for organizational purpose than for the organization's leadership per se.

Let us now consider some of Capra's thoughts more directly. According to Capra and other physicists, matter at the subatomic level does not exist in terms of "things" but as "probability waves." They only *tend* to exist. Those terms that we learned in high school, *protons* and *neutrons*, the subparts of an atom, are not parts, particles, or tangible things as we normally think of them. They may be conceived of as entities but only as a convenience. Capra's own words may help:

Depending on how we look at them, they appear sometimes as particles, sometimes as waves. This dual aspect
of matter was extremely puzzling. The picture of a wave
that is always spread out in space is fundamentally different from the picture of a particle, which implies a sharp
location.

The apparent contradiction was finally resolved in a
completely unexpected way that dealt a blow to the very
foundation of the mechanistic world view — the concept
that matter is real. At the subatomic level, it was found,
matter does not exist with certainty at definite pinpoint-
able places but rather shows "tendencies to exist." These
tendencies are expressed in quantum theory as probabilities, and the corresponding mathematical quantities take
the form of waves; they are similar to the mathematical
forms used to describe, for instance, a vibrating guitar string
or sound wave. This is why particles can be waves at the
same time. They are not "real" three-dimensional waves
like sound waves or water waves. They are "probability
waves," abstract mathematical quantities related to the
probabilities of finding the particles at certain points in
space and at particular times.

At the atomic level, then, the solid-material objects of
classical physics dissolve into wavelike patterns of probabilities. These patterns, furthermore, do not represent
probabilities of things, but rather probabilities of intercon-
nections. (Capra, 1977: p. 22)*

Capra is therefore discussing *relations* of abstract particles.
These relations constitute a unified whole. This kind of thinking
suggested to me that I should consider more directly and dili-
gently the web (to use Capra's term) of relations in organizations.
It is this web, the interactions, the interfaces, that make up or at
least define the total system more clearly than the units and individuals that form the connecting points. For me, this way of
conceiving and diagnosing a system depicts the reality of organizational behavior more closely than other models.

---

*Reprinted by permission from "The Tao of Physics: Reflection on the
'Cosmic Dance,'" by F. Capra. *Saturday Review*, 1977, 5(6).

Jantsch, basing much of his theorizing on the prior work of Prigogine, states that to understand the evolution of living things, one must concentrate more on disequilibrium than on equilibrium. The former, he contends, is far more natural, affirmative, and central to growth and change. To achieve equilibrium is to gain comfort, yet this victory may bring us closer to stagnation and death than to vibrancy and life. Jantsch also holds that evolution is accelerating just as the overall process of change appears to be.

His theory has been heralded by some as a paradigmatic shift comparable to Einstein's move away from Newton. Just as Einstein's theory of relativity wrested the physical sciences away from Newton's static ideas of gravity, Jantsch's ideas challenge us to view movement, relativity, and change in living systems as *constant*. He argues that all living things are always co-evolving yet maintaining a "relativity" to one another. Both Jantsch and Prigogine believe that the disequilibrium and perturbation that occur from time to time in living things are actually a kind of "molting," a shedding of the old within organisms as they strive to attain a higher level of existence. These perturbations, activities of disequilibrium, are signs of positive change that lead to self-organization rather than to decline. Thus, out-of-the-ordinary events may be more significant for organizational understanding than ordinary ones.

A related principle from general systems theory is the idea of the steady state and dynamic homeostasis (see Goodwin Watson's article [1966] for an analysis of resistance to change within this theoretical context). According to this principle, open systems to survive must maintain a steady state. However, a steady state is not motionless or a true equilibrium. As Katz and Kahn (1978) characterize this principle for organizations, "There is a continuous inflow of energy from the external environment and a continuous export of the products of the system, the ratio of the energy exchanges and the relations between parts, remains the same." Even though their theory contends that the steady state is not motionless, Katz and Kahn do note that "relations between parts remain the same" and they conclude that "The basic principle is the preservation of the character of the system." Perhaps their interpretation of general systems theory and

Jantsch's thinking are not that different. Perhaps it is a matter of emphasis.

But it may be that practitioners of OD have overly emphasized the client's achieving a steady state and equilibrium. Yes, OD is at heart identified with change, yet one of our major interventions, team building, is more often than not a striving toward greater equilibrium. ("Let's learn to work better together; let's learn to trust: let's build a more cohesive unit.") These equilibrating goals are worthy, but if OD practitioners spend all their consulting time in this manner and in resolving conflicts, they may be helping to squash needed perturbations and disequilibrium.

Life cycle theory of organizations is pertinent to this last point (see, for example, Greiner, 1972). Usually for an organization to move successfully from one state of the cycle to another, wrenching changes have to be made even to the point of modifying the basic character of the organization.

To summarize, theory from sources other than the ones I usually turn to has challenged my way of understanding and diagnosing organizations. These ideas about matter and living things have stimulated me to concentrate more on the relationships between people and units rather than necessarily the individuals and units per se, and on unusual events rather than on routine operations.

Let me now call attention to some findings and different emphases from the world of practice that have influenced my outlook.

Practice

Some recent studies in management have further influenced my thinking about the importance of relationships and interfaces. We shall consider these studies in four different domains of relationships: 1) the manager's relationships with subordinates, 2) the manager's relationship with his or her boss, 3) the manager's lateral relationships, and 4) the manager's unit's relationships with other individuals and units.

Managing Subordinate Relationships. There is mounting evidence that, used appropriately, a participative management approach pays off. For example, some recent research reveals that managers who move rapidly up the hierarchy tend to involve their subordinates in decision making more than do managers who move up less rapidly. These faster-rising managers were rated by themselves and their subordinates as having a participative style, whereas less successful managers were rated as having a persuasive, "selling" style or one that we might characterize as laissez-faire (Hall, 1976).

In a study of executive competence in a large federal agency, those executives who were widely considered the most competent tended to manage more collaboratively, communicate more openly, solicit information from subordinates more frequently, more often establish trust and mutual respect with subordinates, provide more opportunities for subordinates to express their objections and disagreements with their superior's proposed actions or decisions, and manage work group meetings in ways to ensure that a frank and open exchange of ideas occur (Burke and Myers, 1982). There were at least sixteen other significant differences between the most competent executives and those who were less so. The six I have cited sound to me like a partial role description of a participative manager. In any case, the other behaviors were related to and supportive of the six above.

Blake and Mouton (1982) have also recently provided further theoretical support for their advocacy of 9,9 or participative management as well as some indirect empirical evidence.

Moreover, as pointed out in a *Fortune* magazine article (Saporito, 1986), it seems quite clear now that participative management works (also see Sashkin, 1984); what prevents this form of management becoming more pervasive in spite of the evidence, according to the magazine reporter, is managers' reluctance to share power. As one senior executive put it, "It's no fun if *you* can't make the right decisions" (Saporito, 1986: p. 60).

While I believe that the overall pattern of evidence respecting executive competence leans more and more toward participative management, my point here is not to debate the issue of management style. I *do* wish to emphasize that management is becoming more and more a reciprocal process and less and less a top-down, boss-to-subordinate, one-way street. If reciprocal relationships are a crucial ingredient of management competence, then my job as a consultant is to facilitate reciprocity, to mediate a two-way street, in other words, to work *in between*.

Managing Up. We have some findings about the importance of learning how to influence one's boss. Failure to "manage up," to relate in an active rather than passive way with one's superior, can readily lead to grave problems in the organization if not outright dismissal of a subordinate. Gabarro and Kotter (1980) advise that one should learn quickly the boss's personal and organizational goals, strengths and limitations, work habits and preferences, as well as one's own patterns and style and how they fit with the boss's. The more one knows about these subjects the more influential one is likely to be.

In the aforementioned study of federal executives, we found that three competencies in this domain are critical: the executive's 1) going to bat for subordinates with his or her superiors, 2) being able to present bad news upward in a strategic way, and 3) establishing good relations with upper-level executives.

OD consultants can help subordinates sharpen their abilities to influence upwardly in the hierarchy. Helping subordinates to disclose threatening news, for example, will ensure that a boss is never surprised (a sin). Likewise, knowing how to deflect one's boss from his or her preferred path is no small feat, yet it is often critical to organizational effectiveness. The point, once again, is to work *in between*.

Managing Lateral Relationships. Another set of competencies important to federal executives is skill at managing relationships with outside contractors and with other units within their organization. Moreover, a recent intensive study of successful general managers in the private sector found that the ability and energy to maintain contact with many people (in the hundreds) in their organization was key to their effectiveness (Kotter, 1982). The managers knew an amazing number of people throughout the organization on a first-name basis, and they made frequent use of these relationships to be effective in their work. Maintaining a network is therefore highly significant to the success of a general manager just as it is to the politician.

What struck me about these findings is, of course, the importance of multiple relationships, of establishing as well as maintaining them. In the federal agency study, we labeled one set of the competencies (about a sixth of the total) "influence management" since they were all concerned with the executive's ability to influence others by means other than formal authority. It is perhaps in this domain of management in particular, and organizational functioning in general, that Capra's "web of relations" becomes more salient. The consultant's being able to perceive this web in all its intricacy is central to a good diagnosis and vital to constructive intervention.

Managing Unit Interfaces. In an important paper about the dilemmas of managing by participation, Kanter (1982) treats the matter of linking teams with their environment. This linkage consists of six dilemmas:

1. "You had to be there" — *problems of turnover.* A major outcome of good team building is an increase in member participation accompanied by a lift in team spirit. This same *spirit* becomes a problem when new members join the team, especially if a newcomer happens to be a new boss. The boss can undercut the groups' work or lead the team in unwanted directions. If the team is to remain effective, these new and changing relationships must be managed.

2. The *fixed decision problem.* When a group first begins to operate participatively so that a new team starts to emerge, certain ground rules, norms, and policies gradually become decisions. Later, when membership changes, the new members do not necessarily feel bound by these decisions since they took no part in framing them. Moreover, since all team members should have influence, prior decisions should not be viewed as immutable, the new members might argue. The dilemma, then, is how to continue the process of participation yet not to be obliged continually to renegotiate the team's earlier decisions.

3. *Suboptimization* — too much team spirit. A team can become so preoccupied with itself that its members lose sight of the team's role and function within the larger organization.

4. *Stepping on toes* and territories — the problem of power.

There may be other constituencies within the overall organization who believe that they have a stake in the problem or issue
that the team holds as their exclusive domain. The team feels
that it has worked so well together on this problem or issue that
no one else is qualified to understand it as well, much less to deal
with it effectively. With this knowledge and spirit comes a feeling
of power that may be difficult to share when it is clear that others
outside the team need to be involved.

    5. "N.I.H." (not invented here) — the problem of *owner-
ship and transfer*. It is a commonplace that individuals and organizational units want to do things in their own way. And the
greater the team spirit, the more reluctant members may be to
adopt someone else's ideas, especially another team's. This reluctance, however, may lead to the waste of "reinventing the
wheel" and of not cooperating, say, in the sharing of information.
Diffusion of innovation is one of the most difficult problems of
organizations.

    6. "A time to live and a time to die." Although the evi-
dence is not yet conclusive, there is some indication that participation needs regular renewal. Members of intensive participation groups, such as quality circles and semiautonomous work
teams, have experienced burnout after eighteen months of activity. Periods of interpersonal intensity should alternate with periods of distance. This suggests that some old teams need to die
and new ones formed in their place. With other kinds of groups
and teams, such as task forces, boards, councils, and so on, perhaps it is best to rotate membership rather than kill off old teams
and start anew. Kanter's point is that it is necessary for management to find ways to sustain continuity of participation as members of groups and as units come and go.

    Kanter covers other dilemmas of management participa-
tion, especially within teams themselves and in leader-member
relationships. Her dilemmas concerning a team's linkage with its
environment are particularly pertinent to areas of relationships
and interfaces that OD practitioners may overlook. Flushed with
the success of a team-building effort, the consultant may be blind
to the greater need of helping the team with 1) new members, 2)
perhaps a new leader, 3) other units that may have a stake in some

of the outcomes of the team's work, and 4) its own team members over time, since the need for renewal will emerge sooner than one might expect.

Kanter's dilemmas of managing participation, particularly those dealing with a team and its environment, represent fertile ground for OD consultation, and further illustrate that the ground for consultation is composed largely of relationships and interfaces.

Summary and Conclusions

While I have usually been clear about the person in the client organization with whom I should contract for OD consultation, I have not always been clear that my *ultimate* client was the same person, or his or her boss, or a specific organizational unit such as the top management group, or the total system. It seems to me that other OD consultants are likewise somewhat perplexed about the identity of their ultimate client. As I read works about living systems and reflect on OD practice, I conclude that my ultimate client is that *behavior* in organizations represented by *interactions*, by relationships and interfaces. These interactions represent the basic reality of organizational life and therefore my consultation should concentrate on them. Furthermore, I should pay special attention to nonroutine events of organizational life, since these occurrences generate energy among members to return the system to a steady state, to achieve homeostasis and equilibrium. It is this use of energy and its direction that will tell me more about how the organization really operates than the energy that the members of the organization expend to maintain normal, daily operations. Just as Kurt Lewin observed that the best way to diagnose an organization is to attempt to change it, we may also state that it is easier to understand an organization when it is disturbed by untypical events than when it is operating as usual.

It is not my contention that one should entirely ignore everyday routine, the organizational structure with its boxes and lines, individuals, work units, the president, and the board of directors. It is more a matter of emphasis for me to focus especially on the in-between. I also believe that relationships and interfaces in organizations will grow even more important in the future because of the changing nature of authority, insofar as authority becomes more of a function of expertise and knowledge rather than position, and of the increasing degrees of complexity in managing organizations. It is virtually impossible for a single individual to know a considerable amount, much less everything, about running an organization or even a part of it. This is especially true of high-technology organizations, public or private. Thus, mutual dependency is more the rule than the exception.

Because OD practitioners are knowledgeable about interpersonal process and are skillful in dealing with relationships, there will be plenty of opportunity for constructive work, changing cultures and applying OD in new ways. We simply must become clearer about the true subject (in my term, *client*) of that work.

Bibliography

Ackoff, R. L. 1981. *Creating the Corporate Future* New York: Wiley.

Allport, G. W. 1945. *The Nature of Prejudice.* Reading, Mass.: Addison-Wesley.

Argyris, C. 1962. *Interpersonal Competence and Organizational Effectiveness.* Homewood, Ill.: Dorsey Press.

———. 1968. "Some Unintended Consequences of Rigorous Research." *Psychological Bulletin* 7:185–97.

———. 1970. *Intervention Theory and Method.* Reading, Mass.: Addison-Wesley.

———. 1971. *Management and Organizational Development.* New York: McGraw-Hill.

———. 1973. "The CEO's Behavior: Key to Organizational Development." *Harvard Business Review* 51(2):55–64.

Argyris, C., and D. A. Schön. 1978. *Organizational Learning: A Theory of Action Perspective.* Reading, Mass.: Addison-Wesley.

"At Emery Air Freight: Positive Reinforcement Boosts Performance." *Organizational Dynamics* 1(3):41–67.

Beckhard, R. 1967. "The Confrontation Meeting." *Harvard Business Review* 45(2):149–55.

———. 1969. *Organization Development: Strategies and Models*. Reading, Mass.: Addison-Wesley.

Beckhard, R., and R. T. Harris. 1987. 2nd Edition. *Organizational Transitions: Managing Complex Change*. Reading, Mass.: Addison-Wesley.

Beckhard, R., and D. G. Lake. 1971. "Short- and Long-Range Effects of a Team Development Effort." In *Social Interventions: A Behavioral Science Approach*, edited by H. A. Hornstein, B. B. Bunker, W. W. Burke, M. Gindes, and R. J. Lewicki. New York: Free Press, pp. 421–39.

Beer, M. 1980. *Organization Change and Development*. Santa Monica, Calif.: Goodyear.

Bennis, W. G. 1959. "Leadership Theory and Administrative Behavior." *Administrative Science Quarterly* 4:259–301.

———. 1966. "The Coming Death of Bureaucracy." *Think* (November-December):30–35.

———. 1967. "Organizations of the Future." *Personnel Administration* (September-October):6–19.

———. 1969. *Organization Development: Its Nature, Origins, and Prospects*. Reading, Mass.: Addison-Wesley.

———. 1970. "A Funny Thing Happened on the Way to the Future." *American Psychologist* 25:595–608.

Berkowitz, N. H. 1969. "Audiences and Their Implications for Evaluation Research." *Journal of Applied Behavioral Science* 5:411–28.

Bernstein, W. M., and W. W. Burke. In press. "A Method for Discerning Organizational Meaning Systems: A Diagnostic Aid to the OD Practitioner."

Bion, W. R. 1961. *Experiences in Groups*. New York: Basic Books.

Blake, R. R., and J. S. Mouton. 1964. *The Managerial Grid*. Houston: Gulf.

———. 1968a. *Corporate Excellence through Grid Organization Development*. Houston: Gulf.

———. 1968b. *Corporate Excellence Diagnosis.* Austin, Texas: Scientific Methods.

———. 1978. *The New Managerial Grid.* Houston: Gulf.

———. 1981. *Toward Resolution of the Situationalism vs. "One Best Style ... " Controversy in Leadership Theory, Research, and Practice.* Austin, Texas: Scientific Methods.

———. 1982. "A Comparative Analysis of Situationalism and 9,9 Management by Principle." *Organizational Dynamics* 10(4):20–43

Blake, R. R., J. S. Mouton, L. B. Barnes, and L. E. Greiner. 1964. "Breakthrough in Organizational Development." *Harvard Business Review* 42:133–55.

Bowers, D. G. 1973. "OD Techniques and Their Results in 23 Organizations: The Michigan ICL Study." *Journal of Applied Behavioral Science* 9:21–43.

Bragg, J. E., and I. R. Andrews. 1973. "Participative Decision Making: An Experimental Study in a Hospital." *Journal of Applied Behavioral Science* 9: 727–35.

Brown, L. D. 1972. "Research Action: Organizational Feedback, Understanding, and Change." *Journal of Applied Behavioral Science* 8: 696–711.

Burck, G. 1965. "Union Carbide's Patient Schemers." *Fortune* (December):147–49.

Burke, W. W. 1974. "Managing Conflict between Groups." In *New Technologies in Organizational Development: Vol. 2,* edited by J. D. Adams. San Diego: University Associates, pp. 255–68.

———. 1976. "Organization Development in Transition." *Journal of Applied Behavioral Science* 12:22–43.

———. 1982. *Organization Development: Principles and Practices.* Boston: Little, Brown.

Burke, W. W., L. P. Clark, and C. Koopman. 1984. "Improve Your OD Project's Chances for Success." *Training and Development Journal* 38(8):62–68.

Burke, W. W., and H. A. Hornstein, eds. 1972. *The Social Technology of Organization Development.* La Jolla, Calif.: University Associates.

Burke, W. W., and W. H. Schmidt, 1971. "Primary Target for Change: The Manager of the Organization?" In *Social Intervention: A Behavioral Science Approach*, edited by H. A. Hornstein, B. B. Bunker, W. W. Burke, M. Gindes, and R. J. Lewicki. New York: The Free Press, pp. 373–85.

Burns, T., and G. Stalker. 1961. *The Management of Innovation*. London: Tavistock.

Cameron, K. 1980. "Critical Questions in Assessing Organizational Effectiveness." *Organizational Dynamics* 9(2):66–80.

Capra, F. 1977. "The Tao of Physics: Reflections on the 'Cosmic Dance'." *Saturday Review* 5(6):21–23, 28.

———. 1983. *The Tao of Physics: An Exploration of the Parallels between Modern Physics and Eastern Mysticism*. 2nd ed. Boulder, Colo.: Shambhala Publications.

Chandler, A. 1962. *Strategy and Structure*. Cambridge, Mass.: MIT Press.

Coch, L., and J. R. P. French. 1948. "Overcoming Resistance to Change." *Human Relations* 1:512–32.

Collier, J. 1945. "United States Indian Administration as a Laboratory of Ethnic Relations." *Social Research* 12(May):275–76.

Davis, S. A. 1967. "An Organic Problem-Solving Method of Organizational Change." *Journal of Applied Behavioral Science* 3:3–21.

Deal, T. E., and A. A. Kennedy. 1982. *Corporate Cultures: The Rites and Rituals of Corporate Life*. Reading, Mass.: Addison-Wesley.

Dowling, W. F. 1975. "System 4 Builds Performance and Profits." *Organizational Dynamics* 3(3):23–38.

Duvall, S., and R. A. Wicklund. 1972. *A Theory of Objective Self Awareness*. New York: Academic Press.

Foltz, J. A., J. B. Harvey, and J. McLaughlin. 1974. "Organization Development: A Line Management Function." In *Theory and Method in Organization Development: An Evolutionary Process*, edited by J. D. Adams. Arlington, Va.: NTL Institute, pp. 183–210.

Franklin, J. L. 1976. "Characteristics of Successful and Unsuccessful Organization Development." *Journal of Applied Behavioral Science* 12:471–92.

French, W. L. 1969. "Organization Development: Objectives, Assumptions, and Strategies." *California Management Review* 12:23–34.

French, W. L., and C. H. Bell, Jr. 1978. *Organization Development*, 2nd ed. Englewood Cliffs, N.J.: Prentice-Hall.

Friedlander, F. 1970. "The Primacy of Trust as a Facilitator of Further Group Accomplishment." *Journal of Applied Behavioral Science* 6:387–400.

————. 1976. "OD Reaches Adolescence: An Exploration of Its Underlying Values." *Journal of Applied Behavioral Science* 12(1):7–21.

Frohman, M. A., M. Sashkin, and M. J. Kavanagh. 1976. "Action Research as Applied to Organization Development." *Organization and Administrative Sciences* 7:129–42.

Gabarro, J. J., and J. P. Kotter. 1980. "Managing Your Boss." *Harvard Business Review* 58(1):92–100.

Galbraith, J. R. 1977. *Organization Design*. Reading, Mass.: Addison-Wesley.

Greiner, L. E. 1972. "Evolution and Revolution as Organizations Grow." *Harvard Business Review* 50(4):37–46.

Golembiewski, R. T., K. Billingsley, and S. Yeager. 1976. "Measuring Change and Persistence in Human Affairs: Types of Change Generated by OD Designs." *Journal of Applied Behavioral Science* 12:133–57.

Golembiewski, R. T, R. Hilles, and M. S. Kagno. 1974. "A Longitudinal Study of Flex-time Effects: Some Consequences of an OD Structural Intervention." *Journal of Applied Behavioral Science* 10:503–32.

Goodman, P. S., and J. M. Pennings. 1980. "Critical Issues in Assessing Organizational Effectiveness." In *Organizational Assessment: Perspectives on the Measurement of Organizational Behavior and the Quality of Work Life*, edited by E. E. Lawler, D. A. Nadler, and C. Camman. New York: Wiley-Interscience, pp. 185–215.

Hackman, J. R., and G. R. Oldham, 1975. "Development of the Job Diagnostic Survey." *Journal of Applied Psychology* 60:159–70.

Hall, J. 1976. "To Achieve or Not: The Manager's Choice." *California Management Review* 18(4):5–18.

Harvey, J. B. 1974. "The Abilene Paradox: The Management of Agreement." *Organizational Dynamics* 3 (Summer):63–80.

———. 1977. "Consulting during Crises of Agreement." In *Current Issues and Strategies in Organization Development*, edited by W. W. Burke. New York: Human Sciences Press, pp. 160–86.

Hautaluoma, J. E., and J. F. Gavin. 1975. "Effects of Organizational Diagnosis and Intervention on Blue-Collar 'Blues'." *Journal of Applied Behavioral Science* 11:475–96.

Heisler, W. J. 1975. "Patterns of OD in Practice." *Business Horizons* (February):pp. 77–84.

Herzberg, F. 1966. *Work and the Nature of Man.* Cleveland: World.

Herzberg, F., B. Mausner, and B. Snyderman. 1959. *The Motivation to Work.* New York: Wiley.

Homans, G. C. 1950. *The Human Group.* New York: Harcourt, Brace.

Hornstein, H. A., B. B. Bunker, W. W. Burke, M. Gindes, and R. J. Lewicki. 1971. *Social Interventions: A Behavioral Science Approach.* New York: Free Press.

Hornstein, H. A., and N. M. Tichy. 1973. *Organization Diagnosis and Improvement Strategies.* New York: Behavioral Science Associates.

Huse, E. F., and M. Beer. 1971. "Eclectic Approach to Organizational Development." *Harvard Business Review* 49(5):103–12.

Jantsch, E. 1980. *The Self-Organizing Universe: Scientific and Human Implications of the Emerging Paradigm of Evolution.* Elmsford, N.Y.: Pergamon Press.

Jones, J. E. 1980. "Quality Control of OD Practitioners and Practice." In *Trends and Issues in OD: Current Theory and Practice*, edited by W. W. Burke and L. D. Goodstein. San Diego: University Associates, pp. 333–45.

Kahn, R. I. 1974. "Organizational Development: Some Problems and Proposals." *Journal of Applied Behavioral Science* 10:485–502.

Kanter, R. M. 1982. "Dilemmas of Managing Participation." *Organizational Dynamics* 11(1):5–27.

———. 1984. *The Change Masters: Innovation for Productivity in the American Corporation.* New York: Simon and Schuster.

Katz, D., and R. L. Kahn. 1978. *The Social Psychology of Organizations*, 2nd ed. New York: Wiley.

Kimberly, J. R., and W. R. Nielsen. 1975. "Organization Development and Change in Organizational Performance." *Administrative Science Quarterly* 20:191–206.

King, A. 1974. "Expectation Effects in Organizational Change." *Administrative Science Quarterly* 19:221–30.

King, D. C., J. J. Sherwood, and M. R. Manning. 1978. "OD's Research Base: How to Expand and Utilize It." In *The Cutting Edge: Current Theory and Practice in Organization Development*, edited by W. W. Burke. La Jolla, Calif.: University Associates, pp. 133–48.

Kolb, D., and A. Frohman. 1970. "An Organization Development Approach to Consulting." *Sloan Management Review* 12(1):51–65.

Kotter, J. P. 1982. *The General Managers*. New York: The Free Press.

Lawler, E. E. III 1973. *Motivation in Work Organizations*. Monterey, Calif.: Brooks/Cole.

——. 1977. "Reward Systems." In *Improving Life at Work*, edited by J. R. Hackman and J. L. Suttle. Santa Monica, Calif.: Goodyear, pp. 163–226.

Lawrence, P. R., and J. W. Lorsch, 1967. *Organization and Environment: Managing Differentiation and Integration*. Boston: Division of Research, Harvard Business School.

——. 1969. *Developing Organizations: Diagnosis and Action*. Reading, Mass.: Addison-Wesley.

Levinson, H. 1972a. *Organizational Diagnosis*. Cambridge, Mass.: Harvard University Press.

——. 1972b. "The Clinical Psychologist as Organizational Diagnostician." *Professional Psychology* 3:34–40.

——. 1975. *Executive Stress*. New York: Harper & Row.

Lewicki, R. J., and C. P. Alderfer. 1973. "The Tensions between Research and Intervention in Intergroup Conflict." *Journal of Applied Behavioral Science* 9(4):423–68.

Lewin, K. 1936. *Principles of Topological Psychology*. New York: McGraw-Hill.

——. 1946. "Action Research and Minority Problems." *Journal of Social Issues* 2:34–46.

——. 1948. *Resolving Social Conflicts*. New York: Harper & Brothers.

——. 1951. *Field Theory in Social Science*. New York: Harper & Brothers.

————. 1958. "Group Decision and Social Change." In *Readings in Social Psychology*, edited by E. E. Maccoby, T. M. Newcomb, and E. L. Hartley. New York: Holt, Rinehart, and Winston, pp. 197–211.

Likert, R. 1961. *New Patterns of Management.* New York: McGraw-Hill.

————. 1967. *The Human Organization.* New York: McGraw-Hill.

Lippitt, R., and G. Lippitt. 1975. "Consulting Process in Action." *Training and Development Journal* 29(5):48–54; 29(6):38–44.

Lippitt, R., J. Watson, and B. Westley. 1958. *Dynamics of Planned Change.* New York: Harcourt, Brace.

Lodahl, T. M., and L. K. Williams. 1978. "An Opportunity for OD: The Office Revolution." *OD Practitioner* 10(4):9–11.

Lundberg, C. C., and A. P. Raia. 1976. "Issues in the Practice of Organizational Development Consultancy." *Proceedings of the Annual Meeting of the Academy of Management*, pp. 190–95.

Maccoby, M. 1976. *The Gamesman: The New Corporate Leaders.* New York: Irvington.

McGregor, D. 1960. *The Human Side of Enterprise.* New York: McGraw-Hill.

————. 1967. *The Professional Manager.* New York: McGraw-Hill.

Mann, F. C. 1957. "Studying and Creating Change: A Means to Understanding Social Organization." In *Research in Industrial Human Relations.* Industrial Relations Research Association, Publication No. 17.

Marrow, A. J. 1969. *The Practical Theorist.* New York: Basic Books.

Marrow, A. J., D. G. Bowers, and S. E. Seashore. 1967. *Management by Participation.* New York: Harper & Row.

Maslow, A. H. 1954. *Motivation and Personality.* New York: Harper & Brothers.

————. 1965. *Eupsychian Management: A Journal.* Homewood Ill.: Richard I. Irwin, and the Dorsey Press.

Mayo, E. 1933. *The Human Problems of an Industrial Civilization.* Boston: Harvard University Graduate School of Business.

Morrison, P. 1978. "Evaluation in OD: A Review and an Assessment." *Group and Organization Studies* 3:42–70.

Nadler, D. A. 1977. *Feedback and Organization Development: Using Data-Based Methods.* Reading, Mass.: Addison-Wesley.

———. 1981. "Managing Organizational Change: An Integrative Approach." *Journal of Applied Behavioral Science* 17(2):191–211.

Nadler, D. A., and M. L. Tushman. 1977. "A Diagnostic Model for Organization Behavior." In *Perspectives on Behavior in Organizations,* edited by J. R. Hackman, E. E. Lawler, and L. W. Porter. New York: McGraw-Hill, pp. 85–100.

Naisbett, J. 1982. *Megatrends: Ten New Directions Transforming Our Lives.* New York: Warner Books.

Naisbett, J., and P. Aburdene. 1985. *Re-inventing the Corporation.* New York: Warner Books.

Nicolis, G., and I. Prigogine. 1977. *Self-Organization in Nonequilibrium Systems: From Dissipative Structures to Order through Fluctuations.* New York: Wiley-Interscience.

Pate, L. E., W. R. Nielsen, and P. C. Bacon. 1977. "Advances in Research on Organization Development: Toward a Beginning." *Group and Organization Studies* 2:449–60.

Peters, T. J. 1987. "Whither a Passion for Excellence — Update." *Academy of Management Executive* 1.

Peters, T. J., and R. H. Waterman, Jr. 1982. *In Search of Excellence: Lessons from America's Best-Run Companies.* New York: Harper & Row.

Pfeiffer, J. W., and J. E. Jones. 1978. "OD Readiness." In *The Cutting Edge: Current Theory and Practice in Organization Development,* edited by W. W. Burke. La Jolla, Calif.: University Associates, pp. 179–85.

Porras, J. I. 1979. "The Comparative Impact of Different OD Techniques and Intervention Intensities." *Journal of Applied Science* 15:156–78.

Porras, J. I., and K. Patterson. 1979. "Assessing Planned Change." *Group and Organization Studies* 4:39–58.

Porras, J. I., and A. Wilkens. 1980. "Organization Development in a Large System: An Empirical Assessment." *Journal of Applied Behavioral Science* 16:506–34.

Rice, A. K. 1958. *Productivity and Social Organizations: The Ahmedabad Experiment.* London: Tavistock.

Rioch, M. J. 1970. "The Work of Wilfred Bion on Groups." *Psychiatry* 33:56–66.

Roethlisberger, F. J., and W. J. Dickson. 1939. *Management and the Worker: An Account of a Research Program Conducted by the Western Electric Company.* Cambridge, Mass.: Harvard University Press.

Rogers, C. R. 1968. "Interpersonal Relationships: U.S.A. 2000." *Journal of Applied Behavioral Science* 4:265–80.

Rosenthal, R. 1976. *Experimenter Effects in Behavioral Research,* enlarged ed. New York: Halsted Press.

Rubin, I. 1967. "Increasing Self-Acceptance: A Means of Reducing Prejudice." *Journal of Personality and Social Psychology* 5:233–38.

Saparito, B. 1986. "The Revolt against 'Working Smarter'." *Fortune* 114(2):58–65.

Sashkin, M. 1984. "Participative Management Is an Ethical Imperative." *Organizational Dynamics* 12(4):4–22.

Schein, E. H. 1980. *Organizational Psychology.* 3rd ed. Englewood Cliffs, N.J.: Prentice-Hall.

———. 1985. *Organizational Culture and Leadership.* San Francisco: Jossey-Bass.

———. 1987. *Process Consultation Volume II.* Reading, Mass.: Addison-Wesley.

Schein, E. H., and W. G. Bennis. 1965. *Personal and Organizational Change through Group Methods: The Laboratory Approach.* New York: Wiley.

Schroder, M. 1974. "The Shadow Consultant." *Journal of Applied Behavioral Science* 10:579–94.

Seashore, S. E., and D. G. Bowers. 1970. "Durability of Organizational Change." *American Psychologist* 25 (March):227–33.

Selznick, P. 1957. *Leadership in Administration.* New York: Harper & Row.

Shepard, H. A. 1960. "Three Management Programs and the Theory behind Them." In *An Action Research Program for Organization Improvement.* Ann Arbor, Mich.: Foundation for Research on Human Behavior.

Skinner, B. F. 1948. *Walden Two.* New York: Macmillan.

———. 1953. *Science and Human Behavior.* New York: Macmillan.

———. 1971. *Beyond Freedom and Dignity.* New York: Knopf.

Tannenbaum, R., and S. A. Davis. 1969. "Values, Man, and Organizations." *Industrial Management Review* 10(2):67–83.

Taylor, J., and D. G. Bowers. 1972. *The Survey of Organizations: A Machine Scored Standardized Questionnaire Instrument.* Ann Arbor, Mich.: Institute for Social Research.

Tichy, N. M. 1974. "Agents of Planned Social Change: Congruence of Values, Cognitions, and Actions." *Administrative Science Quarterly* 19:164–82.

———. 1983. *Managing Strategic Change: Technical, Political, and Cultural Dynamics.* New York: Wiley.

Tichy, N. M., and M. A. Devanna. 1986. *The Transformational Leader.* New York: Wiley.

Tichy, N. M., H. A. Hornstein, and J. N. Nisberg. 1977. "Organization Diagnosis and Intervention Strategies: Developing Emergent Pragmatic Theories of Change." In *Current Issues and Strategies in Organization Development,* edited by W. W. Burke. New York: Human Sciences Press, pp. 361–83.

Trist, E. 1960. *Socio-technical Systems.* London: Tavistock Institute of Human Relations.

Trist, E., and K. Bamforth. 1951. "Some Social and Psychological Consequences of the Long Wall Method of Goal-Setting." *Human Relations* 4(1):1–8.

Tushman, M. L., and D. A. Nadler. 1978. "Information Processing as an Integrative Concept in Organizational Design." *Academy of Management Review* 3:613–24.

Vroom, V. 1965. *Work and Motivation.* New York: Wiley.

Walton, R. E. 1969. *Interpersonal Peacemaking: Confrontations and Third Party Consultation.* Reading, Mass.: Addison-Wesley.

Watson, G. 1966. "Resistance to Change." In *Concepts for Social Change,* Cooperative Project for Educational Development Series, Vol. 1, edited by G. Watson. Washington, D. C.: National Training Laboratories.

Weisbord, M. R. 1973. "The Organization Development Contract." *OD Practitioner* 5(2):1–4.

———. 1976. "Organizational Diagnosis: Six Places to Look for Trouble with or without a Theory." *Group and Organization Studies* 1:430–47.

———. 1978. *Organizational Diagnosis: A Workbook of Theory and Practice.* Reading, Mass.: Addison-Wesley.